THE GIANT WITHIN US

THE GIANT WITHIN US

Compiled by Anita DuckWorth-Bradshaw

authorHOUSE®

AuthorHouse™ LLC
1663 Liberty Drive
Bloomington, IN 47403
www.authorhouse.com
Phone: 1-800-839-8640

Published by AuthorHouse 05/28/2014

ISBN: 978-1-4969-0305-1 (sc)
ISBN: 978-1-4969-0306-8 (e)

Table of Contents

Foreword

It was with pleasure that I accepted the request to write a Foreword for this book, The Giant Within Us. Firstly: Well done to Lady Anita Duckworth-Bradshaw for her initiative in creating the idea and asking some very brave women to share their stories.

This book will inspire many people who are currently experiencing challenge and hardship in their own lives. It will lift their spirits. It will cause them to sing within their soul, knowing that they are not alone in the challenges they are experiencing. It will help them to believe that they too can rise up from the difficulties facing them to have the life that they dream of.

I live by the motto, Dream It. Believe It. Achieve It. These brave and inspiring women totally embody that motto. Their very moving and honest accounts of their experiences are testimony their belief systems and mindset. I salute you all.

Everyone deserves to enjoy the life they dream of for themselves. Dream big dreams, and never give up on your dream. Believe that you can achieve your dream, and get on with making the often hard choices in your life, that will support you in achieving your dream.

Adèle McLay
Inspirator, Agitator, Motivator ™
Small Business HUGE Success™
Supporting small business entrepreneurs around the world achieve HUGE success!!
W: adelemclay.com
W: smallbusinesshugesuccess.com

Tw: @adelemclay
FB: AdeleMMcLay
FB: SmallBusinessHugeSuccess
Lin: AdeleMcLay
'Life is either a daring adventure or nothing.' Helen Keller
'See yourself living in abundance and you will attract it.' Bob Proctor

Thank you

"I define nothing. Not beauty, not patriotism. I take each thing as it is; Without prior rules about what it should be."

~ Bob Dylan

Not knowing how my potential co-authors would welcome my proposition, I took a chance and today it's a reality.

My deepest gratitude is to my heavenly father, God Almighty, who has given me the creative ability to champion this project and to live in my purpose.

To my husband (George) who shared my fears and my hope whilst piloting this project.

To Virginia Price who has delivered incredibly beautiful pictures for us, including my photo.

To the most beautiful powerhouse Angels (Tope Lawal, Lady Joanne Stewart, Abiodun Titiloye Oluokun, Petrina Kamara, Kim Schuld, Esther Austin, Chris Tuck, Joy Ibibo, Nguavese Amokaha, Rosemary Pharo, Buky Orija, Sandra Nelson, Anne Anouna, Antonetta Fernandes, Zoë A. Onah, Abimbola Betty Oso, Usha Oliver, Maureen Pearson and Sasha Capicco). Thank you for believing in my leadership and for putting your trust in my humble self to sail us safely to our audacious destination. This project would not have been the same without your contribution. I salute you all for taking a chance on me.

To our readers, thank you for investing your time, energy and money to own a copy of this piece.

Introduction

"A runner must run with dreams in his heart, not
money in his pocket."

~ Emil Zatopek

I t all started when an associate approached me to be a part of a project
she was already working on. She also gave me an opportunity to start
my own anthology.

As an entrepreneur and wealth creator, I know when to act upon an
idea and when to say no, and the proposition seemed good enough to
pursue; so I took a chance on it.

What was most inspiring was the opportunity to work with other
incredible individuals to make my idea a reality. I know the power of
cooperative synergy and the difference it would make when the right
individuals are involved in a journey such as this. Having this truth,
the fear of not achieving my goal simply vanished and an inner strength
took hold of me as I began to search for the right partners to support
me to steer this massive ship to its destination.

I started to contact others who had already been down this road before
now. I wondered whether we would pull it off in the stipulated time
from project conception to the commissioning of the finished product.
As a risk taker, I knew there would be no better time than the one I was
given to work on this project.

This book has been written by the most beautiful and incredibly
powerful women of our time. Each one of them had the strength
to rise above every challenge they were faced with. Their stories will

provoke you to take action in order to reach your desired destination. There's only one place you can find true success and that is when world nurturers (women) decide to work together. These women reorganised The Giant within Us (every human being) can be woken up if only we try.

These women have walked the path of life's challenges, but they remain determined never to give up on their resolute to do, have and become more. Today, we are privileged to read some of their stories.

Their stories will educate, inspire and motivate you to never give up on your dreams and goals no matter the road blocks and bumps on your way.

This book will move you to identify opportunities as they come your way. It will encourage you to break out of the smallness and become the giant within.

Change is constant and to do, have and become more; we must embrace it with open arms. Let's not forget that there are two kinds of change (natural and through human influences). The natural changes (seasons and time) cannot be influenced by humans, but our decisions, behaviours and habits can be changed to reflect our deepest desires if we are receptive the endless possibilities that is around us.

Some changes could be negative, whilst most are positive. To bring change we must decide to travel on the journey of discovery. Part of positive change includes personal and professional development. However, the change we all seek lies within each one of us.

Each chapter of this book will indeed bring new hope and possibilities for you to never give up on yourself.

"The Change we seek is within us."
~ Anita Duckworth-Bradshaw

Anita Duckworth-Bradshaw

Anita Duckworth-Bradshaw (popularly known as Anita Bradshaw) is the founder of two international organizations (La Proverbs Ltd and Woman The Powerhouse Ltd) based in London. She is an accredited coach from the Coaching Academy UK. She is an incredible Business and Life coach, motivational speaker and trainer who takes pride in supporting others to do, have and become more.

Coach Anita is the author of two books, *The Road To Discovery* and

Woman The Powerhouse. She also supports charities around the world.

Contact Info:

www.laproverbsacademy.net
www.womanthepowerhouse.com
anita@laproverbsacademy.net
Anita Bradshaw
@laproverbs
Lady Anita Duckworth-Bradshaw

Chapter 1
Life Is Full Of Endless Possibilities

By Anita Duckworth-Bradshaw

D iamonds and other precious stones are usually found in the rough. For them to become valuable, they must go through some tough processes.

Most humans are not interested in the processes of anything or any journey but the end product. What we fail to realize is the fact that learning, growing, transforming, purifying, healing and becoming more happens through processes.

Without taking the precious stones through the fire and the purifying processes, their value remains unknown. The endless possibilities in life lie in the process of our challenges.

Whilst most people would prefer the finished product or being carried to their destination (whereby they lose the essence of being in the now), some of us prefer to go through the process.

A wise man once said, "Let life teach you."

This simply means that in every stage of our lives, whether smooth or rough, there are things to learn from each experience. It's a well-known fact that an average mind would wish things were easy, whilst a great mind explores and assimilates the lessons of each stage of their journey.

In August 1986, at the tender age of seven, I left my family to live with one of my sisters in the city. The epic journey was not a holiday but the beginning of a long learning process and character building for me.

No wonder a wise man said, "Do not be afraid to take risk, for where there's risk comes reward."

Before leaving my family, we were told that my sister had a baby and she specifically requested for me to join them in the city. My responsibility was to look after my beautiful niece and manage chores at home. Sometimes the demand became too much and I wanted to return to my family in the village. However, my choice was to remain in the city to learn how to become more and change my current situation. The joy of being in the city and not in the village was my awakening period and I learned so much during that time.

I invested eleven years of my life with my sister, and every day brought new challenges and experiences. My core objective was to remain focused in order for one day become free from being told what to do and being controlled by others without resistance. Life was very tough during those eleven years, and the environment was not encouraging for an ambitious mind such as mine.

As we can't predict the future but can only plan to succeed in our own ways, along came three other beautiful nieces. My role was to ensure their day-to-day activities were well managed. I was 80% responsible for the running of my sister's home whilst she and her husband went out to fend for the family.

Even though life was extremely challenging at that point in time, I chose not to settle with the rest of the people in my environment.

> "Life is 10% what happens to us and 90% how we
> respond to those challenges in our everyday living."
> ~ Anita Duckworth-Bradshaw

Going through the process of not having enough or not living the life of the most fortunate in society does not mean we have to give up. I consciously made up my mind never to give up on my dreams to become somebody someday.

Looking back, I don't think I ever went to bed before 11pm for the entire eleven years of my life at my sister's home. "Someday" was far away during those eleven years, but I believed in my heart that my dreams and desires would eventually become a reality.

Finally, that someday came in 2004 when I got married to the most amazing man in the world. However, between 1997 and 2003, I went through a whole new level of process and learning. They came in different shapes and sizes (independence, relationships, education, rejection, mistakes, loss of my mother and a myriad of life challenges), but I survived them all.

"Let's not forget that for every success, there's a price
to pay."
~ Anita Duckworth-Bradshaw

My move from Nigeria to the UK was another giant leap in my journey of endless possibilities. At that time I didn't know what to expect, but mentally the decision not to settle as an average individual was made a long time before my arrival. I knew poverty and had lived amongst survival of all sorts; my plan was to become a solution provider in my lifetime and nothing short of that. I was not oblivious to the challenges that lay ahead. With this in mind, my every move and the people I chose to spend my time with became very important to me.

One of the toughest decisions I had ever made was to leave my familiar environment and stepped into the unknown. Not having an immediate family in a foreign country was not a walk in the park, but my mind to do, have and become more was already made up.

"Endless possibilities lie in our future.
Our responsibilities are to discover them."
~ Anita Duckworth-Bradshaw

After studying the pattern in my new environment, I decided to work towards discovering my passion for change and place in the society. The best action I took was to invest a large sum of money into my personal and professional development. Through my education, I set up my first company supporting individuals and organizations with business and life coaching, consulting, project management, strategizing and aiding their total transition to creating positive change. As an authority in personal and professional development, I know and believe that every change we desire lays inside each and every one us.

Below are some of the actions that I took in order to attain my personal and professional goals.

- First was the discovery of my passion (coaching, mentoring and teaching others).
- The desire to be in a position to support myself and others
- I embraced change as it came my way
- I set future personal and professional goals
- I moved away from my comfort zone
- I let go of some people and habits
- I invested in my personal and professional development
- I chose to be responsible for my actions

Unfortunately, most people choose **option hope, no goals nor action**. I chose and teach **option hope, goal setting and action.** The reason is that the second option is the practical way to change any circumstance or situation. Let's not forget that every single day of our lives, opportunities knock on our door. The only difference is our ability to recognize and embrace them, which lies within each one of us. Becoming more takes energy, time and money. We are responsible for making those decisions and taking action in order to change our current situation.

> "It's not the blowing of the wind that determines
> your destination, but the setting of sail."
> ~ Jim Rohn

My setting of the sail was to be in a position where I could comfortably provide support to people around the world. With some of the challenges

I had faced in the past (such as not knowing where the next meal was going to come from), I chose to stay in the zone of possibility. Today I'm living my purpose and enjoying the very essence of my being. I would not have done all these without the help of God and the incredible support of my family, especially my husband.

To do, have and become more, these are my suggestions.

I. Discover who you are (your purpose)
II. Set your short-term and long-term goals
III. Take time to plan each step which, if taken, will get you to your desired destination
IV. Take action—once you discover your purpose, take action to locate the right people who would support you on your journey.

You have to learn to associate yourself with people who believe in your dream. As humans, often times we have a lot of pressure from the world (family, job, everything else), and in the process we lose focus of our personal goals. You have all you require to become a better and more powerful you.

This is a chance for you to discover how you want your life to be. Most people are not living their dreams because of fear of rejection and failure. You hold the key to your future and you are the only one who can unlock that giant within.

Everything you discover about yourself will propel you to your destination. It doesn't't matter what you have been through or what you are going through right now. Your purpose cannot be defined by someone else. Stop making excuses and take action.

Whether you are 18 or 80 it makes no difference. You must make a decision to travel on the road to discovering your true self. People of all ages, colours and races allow lack of education, difficult childhood, disappointment and past negative experiences to prevent them from taking bold steps that could lead to endless possibilities.

   I.   Review your goals/action
   II.   Ask for God's help
   III.   Don't be afraid to make mistakes
   IV.   Take risk

Life is indeed full of endless possibilities!

Lady Joanne Stewart

Lady Joanne Stewart, The Life Organiser, is the Founder and Director of Solutions By Lady Jo Ltd.

Lady Jo is a Life Coach and Mentor, Professional Organiser and Virtual Assistant with over 25 years of experience working in high pressured and professional environments.

Having experienced abuse and tragedies in her personal life, Lady Jo made the choice to transform her life and then took the appropriate action to make it happen.

She decided to combine her professional experience, training, knowledge and skills with all the personal hurt to good use and runs her own business as a Life Coach and Mentor and Professional Organiser. She is dedicated to making a positive difference in people's lives, supporting and inspiring others, particularly women, and to show that even in the face of adversity, we all have the power and strength within ourselves to turn our lives around for the better. Using the coaching, mentoring and organising skills Lady Jo can deliver a service, that meets client's needs in a professional, emotional and practical way.

She currently volunteer's with women's groups relating to sexual and domestic violence.

In her private life, Lady Jo is a wife and mum of two children, has a dog and three cats, and her main priority is and has always been her family.

Contact details

Email:	ladyjo2010@iCloud.com
Skype:	ladyjo1606
Website:	http://www.solutionsbyladyjo.com/
Twitter:	@LadyJo1606
Facebook:	www.facebook.com/solutionsbyladyjo
LinkedIn:	http://uk.linkedin.com/pub/lady-joanne-stewart/55/305/649/
Pinterest:	Lady Joanne Stewart

Chapter 2
I turned my life around—so can you!

by Lady Joanne Stewart

If you had told me a few years ago that I would be a qualified life coach and professional organiser, running my own business, writing books, public speaking and would have relocated to a place where I knew nobody, I may have laughed at you, perhaps thought you were insane, but I certainly wouldn't have believed you. However, here I am. I have turned my life around for the better and almost beyond recognition in the last few years.

People began to tell me that I was inspirational; they admired my courage and strength. I hadn't thought about it that way, I was just trying to survive each day. I slowly began to see that I was strong; I was still here and fighting.

I would like to share some of my story with you to demonstrate how I got through, and how you too can turn your life around. I hope that some of my story along with my own quotations that I include in this chapter will potentially motivate, uplift and encourage you to take stock of your life, and make any necessary changes.

Two dates changed my life. The first was 9th May 1989, the second was 7th November 2010. The first led me down a path of depression and years of torment and abuse. The second however, in a sudden moment of clarity, I knew that I had to change my life for the better—immediately.

Having lived for over 20 years with severe depression, aftermath of rape, sexual abuse and domestic abuse, I knew the time had come for change.

To people that have not experienced any form of abuse coupled with depression it may seem obvious. But when you are caught in a vicious cycle of emotion, there is often little clarity.

In these situations there is only one person that you can look to for help and support initially. All the best professionals, well intending, loving, supportive people in the world cannot help you unless and until you decide you are ready to help yourself. There is only so much that others can do in those first moments. You alone must be the one to take action—even if it is a small baby step. It does not need to be a giant leap.

"You can decide to make positive changes in your life even in the toughest, darkest times. Believe in yourself and take that first step."

So just how does one take that first step? Well clearly everybody is an individual; we all have a different story to tell, a different path to tread, so each person's step will be unique to them. But it all stems from how we think.

Everything we do in life is determined by our thoughts, and the choices we make. Our thoughts will determine the kind of day we will have.

It is well documented how people have lived through the toughest times and have stayed remarkably positive.

"Sometimes things can seem fairly bleak, but if you search within yourself, you will find the strength you need to carry on. Don't give up. Things will improve."

Let's take C P, an American pilot serving during the Vietnam War. You may not have heard of him, but his is a tale of remarkable strength of character. Following an air missile strike causing a crash landing of the plane he was flying South of Hanoi, he was captured, tortured and imprisoned for five years and nine months. In interviews he gave after his release he talked of "reaching a fork in the road, you have a scenario that you can cry about or smile about. I've learned it's a whole lot healthier to smile about it."

As a serving officer at that time, he had thought that should the worst happen and he be captured as a prisoner of war that he wouldn't survive. But then he found an inner strength he didn't realise he had which enabled him to cope with the desperate situation he found himself in. He is quoted as saying "I don't mean to minimize the size of your problems by my story. All I mean to say is that just like any other major problems; they are going to be as big or small as you make them by the choices you make."

I believe that the words of this pilot are true. We each face challenges and difficult times in life. We cannot compare the extent of others problems with our own, nor understand the depth of feelings they evoke in us. We are each unique. For some they may have health problems— agonizing, debilitating illness, disability or disease, others grieve the loss of loved ones, poverty, starvation, homelessness, or some like me have lived with abuse and depression for many years. People will have problems in their life that society as a whole may think of as almost irrelevant alongside the infamous "there's always someone worse off".

Whatever your problems and issues are, all of it comes back down to what you think, and your thoughts determine your attitude and your choices you make. Outside influences can unquestionably have dramatic effects on our lives, especially dealing with the loss of a loved one, and we need to take time to process our thoughts.

In life you can choose to be defeated, give up, be miserable and negative just as easily as you can choose to be happy and positive. It is a simple decision we make each day when we wake up. People allow outside influences to lead to negativity, or having a bad day. I have been and on occasion still am guilty of this myself, although much, less these days.

When you receive bad news, you can decide there and then how you will let it affect you. Do you give up? Or do you simply find another way around? If you have an obstacle in your path—tackle it head on and keep working towards your destination.

Just yesterday I received news that at first I was deeply upset about. But I decided to take a few hours to think about it. This morning I have attacked a plan of action with renewed excitement, vigor and energy. I have chosen not to let yesterday's initial disappointment get the better of me. Instead I embrace this fresh opportunity it has presented me with and feel that this will be even better than my original plan. An alternative was I could have felt upset and bitter about it. I could have allowed myself to feel miserable but I chose not to. What avenue would you choose?

> *"As sunrise brings us a brand new day,*
> *it brings with it brand new opportunities.*
> *Are you ready to grasp them with both hands?*
> *Or are you still holding on to yesterday?"*

It is all too easy in this busy world to feel a little overwhelmed or out of control. Life often moves at a fast pace, with many demands placed on us. It is your response to this that is important. It is human nature to worry about things, often when there is no need. There is a very apt Swedish proverb—Worry gives a small thing a big shadow. Our thoughts can often lead to 'worst case scenario', or the big 'what if . . . ?'

Before I had my moment of clarity, I lived my life with many thoughts of what I had been through—the struggle and pain, both emotionally and physically. My past was dictating how I was living each day—I was allowing this to happen. We cannot go back and change anything from our past. We can however choose to change the way we think of the past. It is true that it is easier said than done, but the past is the past. It is gone. What matters is the present, and moving on.

> *"We cannot undo the negative experiences we*
> *have had, but we can choose to learn from them*
> *and move forward with a positive attitude."*

So you've had your moment of clarity, you're ready to take your first step, what's next? How about a de-clutter?

"It is only when we are able to begin to let our past go, that we can truly begin to look to the brighter future we deserve."

De-cluttering goes far beyond having a traditional spring clean in your home. Think of it as letting go. We need to be able to let go of things in order to move forwards in life. From old clothes to old paperwork; and from our thoughts to people. Yes—I did say people! Continuing relationships with people that bring you down, hold you back or are constantly negative can be harmful, and as harsh as it sounds, sometimes letting go of some people is the correct option for you. The same with our thoughts—we need to calm our minds.

"Move negative thoughts out,
be open to positive thinking,
and there will be no stopping you!

Let go.
Change your thoughts.
Change your attitude.
Change your life."

So—what do you need to let go of?

Abiodun Oluokun

Abiodun Oluokun is married and a mum of 2 lovely girls, an infoprenuer, speaker, business and financial intelligence coach. She is the co-founder of the outstanding—NVQMadeSimple website—an online support centre for QCF Learners and the founder of Business Success Class (BSC) where she helps people who desire a change in their financial state to discover a starting point and grows a successful business. She decided to set up her own business and create time and financial freedom to live the life that she desired—a life of giving and full of meaning!

Yookos, Free Membership Group:

www.yookos.com/groups/successfulwomen-in-business
www.businesssuccessclass.com/freegift
www.businesssuccessclass.com
hello@businesssuccessclass.com
facebook.com/BusinessSuccessClass
twitter.com/bsuccessclass

Chapter 3
Anything Is Possible If You Can Change!

By Abiodun Oluokun

I t's amazing when you discover what you enjoy doing and can turn it into a profitable business; however, there are many lessons to learn and it can be a very long and sometimes rough journey when you do it all on your own. This I have experienced first-hand. I have learned a great deal of lessons along the way that you can benefit from to save yourself time and effort in reaching your dream faster!

> "Doing the same thing year in and year out and expecting a different result is insanity."
> ~ Albert Einstein

It's time to change the way we do things, especially when it's not working!

Many years ago, as far back as my childhood years, I had this fascination with making things to sell; I just wanted to make money of my own. I remember as early as the age of 9 I started exploring quite a few options such as knitting small purses to sell to my classmates in primary school. I once took money from my piggy bank at the age of 13, went to the market, bought a bunch of bananas and fried them in oil to make banana chips to sell. Of course you can imagine what happened. It went wrong as the bananas soaked up the oil and I didn't't get my crispy chips to sell. I wasted all the resources, if only I had asked my mum!

When I moved on to secondary school, I gained my first experience selling in an organized environment. I was schooled in a boarding house and the school had only one shop. It was referred to as "The Tuck Shop," which opened once or twice each week. I volunteered to help at the shop and within a short time became a sales leader and was in charge of holding the keys to the shop. I was given the opportunity to run the evenings with a team selling toiletries, stationery, drinks and snacks and also balance the account without losing a kobo. I totally enjoyed counting money, and I thank Mrs. Olasehinde for giving me such an opportunity!

I really didn't't conclude at the time that I loved selling or running a business. When it was time to decide which course to do in university, I concluded that it would be medicine because I loved helping people. We didn't't have career coaches at the time, and every mother's dream for her children was for them to be a doctor, lawyer or an accountant; so I felt I had made a good choice! I did my exams, but did not attain the requisite grades needed to study medicine. I eventually graduated from university with a degree in Child Psychology and Family Counselling. For the four years I studied at university, I plunged into different business ventures—from selling postcards and eggs to making zobo to sell—all of which were profitable ventures. However, little did I know that I was following an innate passion that would stay with me for many years.

> "Without a mentor your very best thinking has got
> you exactly where you are today."
> ~ Raymond Aaron

In the midst of my adventure in university, I found my Mr. Right and he was quite skilful in upgrading our business to generate more revenue, which he still does today. Thank God for good husbands because sometimes it's not just your abilities you need to keep you going as a woman in business. You need a mentor!

I realized this many years afterwards when building my first online business with my husband. In 2008 after attending a business and career seminar, I discovered I had put away a training certificate of mine for two years without exploring what kind of job I could get with it. I heard a testimonial of how someone else had doubled their income at the time just by getting a job with that same type of certificate. I awoke from my slumber, updated my CV and within seven days got a new job that doubled my income. That's what can happen when you attend a business and career seminar; you suddenly realize you can be more than what you are now, you see people who are no different from yourself exploring a better way and you can do it too. A two-week, three-month or one-year course in addition to what you have can make a whole lot of difference. Today, you can complete courses from the comfort of your home; online and through webinars!

> "You can start your own business if you can find a
> game changer in your profession."
> ~ Abiodun oluokun

After a few months in my new job, my passion for having my own business kept finding its way into my career. I had just learned about active and passive income from reading a book and playing a financial game; my job was active income and I was seeking a way to create passive income. I discovered a need in my profession and with the help of my husband I turned my knowledge into a series of E-books to help NVQ Candidates in the health and social care industry. It was called NVQ Made Simple! Every day I worked on the business alongside my job until the revenue from the business was able to pay my salary, then I said goodbye to my full time job and became a freelancer. It really felt good to be free.

> "It is crazy to be going for the trial and error
> approach to business, just get a mentor and follow a
> proven success path."
> ~ Armand Morin

NVQ Made Simple kept growing, and my husband and I got some partners on board. We had weekly meetings with each other, but it wasn't going uphill at the speed we wanted. Three years later the structure of the qualification changed from NVQ to QCF, and I learned another strong lesson—never sit down on a one legged stool; it's the most wicked thing you can do to yourself or your family. If you have a job, it means you have cash flow to create an additional income stream on the side. If you have an existing business that's doing well, it's time to create another income stream. My song changed from creating passive income to creating multiple income streams.

I asked myself a critical question while rebuilding my business all over again: what would I do better this time? I concluded that I need to ASK as many questions as possible from those who have succeeded on the same path. Pay for the knowledge where it is required and have a deep hunger to get things done within the fastest time possible. Some opportunities have expiry dates!

In the process of building my own business, I have found many game changers in my niche and increased my skill set. Over the years I have had the privilege to share my knowledge and support others to turn their passion into a business. I now help others who want to create a business or take their business to the next level or find direction. There is so much information out there and many are already suffering from information overload. What you need is not just more information, but step-by-step instruction to get you to where you want to be. You also need someone to be there for you—a mentor or coach. These are conscious changes I had to make to achieve success in my business.

I believe what you have in your hands is enough to start, but what you know may not be enough. To achieve the results you want to see, you've got to do things in a different way—anything is possible if you can change!

Therefore, I have a complimentary gift I would like you to have as you make a conscious effort to change yourself first and then your business. Pop over to the link below and download your free gift titled *10 Major Steps to Starting Out Rightly in Business.*

The journey you've been through in life is your stepping stone to great victory, and there are lessons to learn before moving on. In every challenge or problem there is an opportunity. It's time to step up and be the best you that ever walked the earth. You can start today!

Chris Tuck

❦

Chris Tuck is the owner of West Wickham Health & Fitness and has helped hundreds of women change their lifestyles, lose weight, get fit, and regain their health and self-confidence.

Chris is an adult survivor of child abuse, and through her own experiences she recognized that by gaining knowledge and expertise in health and fitness, she could overcome her own issues and help others with theirs.

In the face of adversity Chris has triumphed over life and show how others can too.

Chris is the co-founder of Survivors-of-abuse.org and co-creator of the "Breaking the Cycle" C.L.E.A.N. Living Health and Wellness Programmes.

www.christuck.co
www.survivors-of-abuse.org
www.christuckmystory.com
www.westwickhamfitness.com
07932-594712 ctsfitness@hotmail.co.uk
facebook.com/CT.WWHF
twitter.com/ChrisTuck_WWHF

Chapter 4

Mindset, Nutrition & Fitness In Overcoming Trauma

By Chris Tuck

I am Chris Tuck, a Trauma, Health and Fitness Coach, Author, and Childhood Abuse Survivor and Ambassador who transforms my clients' lives by integrating mindset, nutrition, fitness and de-stressing protocols.

Thump thump thump. My heart is banging ten to the dozen in my chest as if it is going to explode. I can feel my blood pumping in my ears. My breathing is shallower and faster. My muscles tighten. My pupils dilate.

My radar is up. My body is alert, ready and waiting.

I'm scared. I'm anxious. All my senses are heightened. I can smell, touch, taste, feel and see what is going to happen . . . again.

I've been here before hundreds of times, in fact. Here comes my abuser.

I'm ready to do whatever it takes to survive.

I might run away. I might freeze and just take what's coming, or TODAY I just might stand my ground and fight.

Is this a real event? A memory, a nightmare? It doesn't matter. The brain sees it the same. It's a threat to my survival.

Even when the threat is not physically there anymore, my body prepares itself for fight, flight or freeze every time. My emotions and feelings have become hard wired into my brain. Unless I deal with the real cause of my anxiety, every little threat can make me react in the same way. I will constantly be living in my reptilian brain space. I will constantly be frightened of my own shadow—walking on eggshells, living a life that serves someone else, not ME.

My body is in sympathetic nervous system dominant mode, and for many abused people it has been this way for years.

In the first 16 years of my life I moved home about 8 times, moved families twice, lived in a tent in Wales for six months and ended up in the local homeless unit three times. I moved schools many times; sometimes I did not go to school. My siblings and I were malnourished, beaten and neglected by the adults that should have been caring for us; and we were bullied by the kids at school. My childhood was the pits—emotionally and physically damaging, especially for my siblings. I became the mum to my two brothers and sister.

After the perceived threat passes, my body slumps and I became very tired. My body craves carbohydrates. Like many abused people I am in a cycle of emotional eating, craving sweets, chocolate, cake—anything that will make me feel good for a moment in time, anything to fill the void, the big black hole in my stomach, in my head. Then the guilt kicks in. I started berating myself. I gained some weight. I felt fat, unloved, unworthy; my self-esteem is at rock bottom. I feel under threat and the cycle continues. I reached for more comfort food.

I developed bulimia to cope with episodes of high stress. Other abuse survivors turn to alcohol, drugs, self-harm or anorexia.

These reactionary behaviours become habitual over time and harm your mental, physical and emotional wellbeing. In 2000 I had a breakdown, and the only way I could turn my life around was to break the cycle of what I was doing. I needed to acknowledge that I had a problem. I needed to understand what was happening to me, and I needed to find a solution to my problem, which is not an easy task when you don't trust anyone, when you are ashamed of whom you are and are afraid about what will happen when you tell!

Through my training as a Trauma and Health Coach, I have learned that in order to maintain good emotional, mental and physical health, we need to de-stress our bodies. We need to live more in our para-sympathetic nervous system, not the sympathetic branch of our nervous system, as many abused people do.

Our para-sympathetic nervous system allows us to rest, digest and regenerate. It allows us to live in our neo-mammalian brain—the frontal lobe that allows us to be at peace with ourselves; it allows us to achieve everything that we want from our lives.

How do we start to move from a chronic stressed state of being to a calm, relaxed and happy state of being?

The easiest way of reclaiming a calm, relaxed and happy state of being and getting rid of the tension in our bodies is by mastering our breathing. Breathing into your belly rather than your chest takes you out of the sympathetic nervous system and into your para-sympathetic nervous system, which means that you rest and your digestion improves; your sleep will improve and your general anxieties will lessen.

Any meal that you eat under stress will not be digested properly; you will not extract all the nutrition out of the food you have eaten. You could be eating the healthiest food every day, but if you are stressed, anxious, worried and angry, you will not be giving your nervous system the best chance to extract the nutrients from the healthy food.

Just a minute a day of simply breathing into your lower belly can help you begin to adjust your system to help you work with yourself, not against yourself.

Try box breathing: breathe in for 4 slow counts and hold it for 4 slow counts, breathe out for 4 slow counts and hold it for 4 slow counts. Repeat for 60 seconds before you go to sleep and before you eat.

My Top 5 Tips

Any change is scary. More often than not it is easier and more comfortable to stay with what you know, even if you are being abused and are miserable. Some people even think that their abuse is "normal" and that they deserve it; they don't know any differently.

I have 5 tips to share with you. They have helped me move on from my abuse.

1. You need to have enough discomfort to want to seek change. You need a deep-rooted reason to make the change because it will help you to succeed. It will help you through those dark, tough times. It will make you commit to the change.
   At the age of 15 I knew that I had to leave home no matter what. I had no money, nowhere to live. However, my discomfort of staying at home outstripped the challenges that lay ahead of me. I needed to leave my childhood abuse behind me. I wanted more. I wanted to be loved, happy and healthy. I wanted security, stability and a family of my own. This is what drove me to succeed and attain everything that I set out to achieve. This changed and evolved as I got older!

2. Speak up/speak out. Find someone you trust to talk to and confide in. It might be a friend, a family member, a stranger or a group like S.O.B., NSPCC, NAPAC or the Samaritans. Do not think that you are alone; there are many people in the world that have been abused. Do not suffer in silence. Take the first step and free yourself from your abuser. Say NO to your abuser and tell someone about your abuse.

3. Be prepared for rejection. Life can be harsh and when you finally have the courage to speak up/speak out you may not be believed. If this is the case, the person you have told is not ready to hear the truth, and they may never be ready! Contact one of

the organisations listed above. They can help you move forward and get you the help that you need.

4. Unburden yourself. Take the necessary actions for you to lead a happy and healthy life. This is your right as a human being. After my breakdown in 2000 I had therapy to help work through my childhood trauma. I was scared and felt ashamed and guilty. I was full of anger and resentment—all of which were making me unwell mentally and physically.

5. Look after yourself. Be kind to yourself, eat nutritious food, learn to de-stress your body, choose an activity that you enjoy and take time out for you!

To help me understand my abuse I read many books, listened to other stories, had therapy and wrote my book. I took small positive steps in the right direction, built up my confidence and went after what I wanted. I have done this through a positive mindset, nutrition and exercise.

I believe that you can achieve anything that you want to. With the help of people like my siblings and me who are openly talking about the damage of abuse, YOU can move forward with your life.

Esther Austin

Esther Austin is a London based multi-faceted empowerment entrepreneur of Barbadian parentage. She is the oldest of three girls, and has two grown sons.

Esther Austin Global has a personal transformation and healing organization. Under this are Qarma Broadcast, Qarma Therapies and Qarma Psychics. Esther is the author of 8 books, a Radio Presenter and Broadcaster, Empowerment Speaker, gifted Intuitive Healer and Intuitive Reader, Life Coach, Hypno-Analysis and Regression Healer.

www.estheraustinglobal.com
07534 508919 info@estheraustinglobal.com

Chapter 5
The Ever Shifting ME: From Pain To Glory

By Esther Austin

So where does my journey start? Where does anyone's journey start? I guess I need to go into my heart space and exhale and see with clarity what comes up. I don't want this story to be one of lament and woe. I want to share the balance of my life as a truth experienced, those poignant and life changing moments, which, like goal posts, have moulded me, fire sharpening iron, sometimes kicking and screaming into becoming who I am now and forming the work I now do.

I remember fleeting episodes from my childhood, realizing on some level that I was different. I know my middle sister (now deceased) felt the same. I always had a deeper sense of knowing, experiencing the world not as a child but seeing it through ancient eyes and perspectives. This is the reason I was usually on my own, as I couldn't't relate to others as I felt that they talked about trivial stuff. I had two sisters— one 18 months younger and another 5 years younger. My parents were deeply religious and incredibly strict.

I spent a lot of time on my own fantasizing and talking to the fairies, having some of the most amazing and sometimes scary spiritual experiences. *Amazing* because I always knew what was going to happen and was able to read people's thoughts and bodies and sense feelings and emotions. *The scary part of my journey is my experience of having visitations at night by other beings.* I remember feeling the bed dip with heaviness and I would keep my head under the covers saying the Lord's

Prayer. Yet; I knew I was connected to another world beyond the one I was in, and that awareness has grown stronger with me until this day.

My journey, like many, has been an eclectic mix of everything the Universe could throw at someone. I have been places where my soul has cried out from the pit of pain as I journeyed, tired and alone (in the physical). My marriage was one of my biggest lessons. I often existed in survival mode in a world of constant criticism and judgment. I found I was giving away my personal power daily whilst trying to hold onto me, which had become a constant struggle. I was trying to do me as best as I could, but it was hurting so much.

I often found myself constantly having to justify the simplest task even down to when I wanted to eat and what I wanted to watch. I was even woken up in the middle of the night for a "telling off." Every aspect of my being was under constant scrutiny, and I spent a lot of time picking myself up, dusting myself off and trying to exhale.

Yet I am such a different person now and in a much healthier place. Did we have some good times? Yes, we did, but those were few and far between, because as soon as I let my guard down, after the cuddles and kisses ended, another lecture would be waiting. Yet through all this, I created a newsletter for mums and arranged meals and outings. I wrote four books in that space of time took myself to college and won an award. I received the Skillset Millennium Award after creating a website, Caribbean Woman—Focus in the Community, dedicated to celebrating women's achievements. When I was asked to be one of the speakers at the BBC Award Ceremony, with my two young boys in tow, I felt honoured because standing on that podium I realized I could do and be anything I wanted to be. Also, watching my two young sons go through every media pack, take out my picture and say, "this is my mum!" felt like winning my own Oscar, and I haven't stopped since.

The next profound experience was with my younger sister, Deborah, who had breast cancer. She was initially diagnosed in 2002. It went into remission, but in 2005 the cancer came back. I was angry and incensed because in my heart I knew she was not going to beat it this time. I immediately went home and wrote a book dedicated to her called

Looking on from the Outside: Sister to Sister from which all proceeds go to the Breast cancer Haven.

My sister died in November 2006. We were very close and seeing someone I loved, the only person who really ever understood me, go through such pain, really did something to my heart. Once again I took action, because I see every experience as a learning curve. I started a blog, and what an amazing experience that was! My blog went viral and people from all over the world contacted me with their stories and journey. When my sister died, the family received such an incredible outpouring of love and heartfelt wishes and cards. The school where she worked as a teacher closed for the day in her honour. I trekked the Inca Trail for Breast Cancer Haven the following year, raising over £2,500. Yet, even that experience was a big lesson for me, because up in the mountains of Peru, I lost the use of my legs intermittently and had to do the trek with a walking stick and walk at the back with doctors. My lesson here was to **let go** of my hurt and pain of losing my sister and to allow people to support me for the first time.

I've also been homeless briefly, had a case at the Old Bailey for rape, and then four years ago when I was away my younger son had an accident and lost a finger. In December 2011 my mother was diagnosed with cancer and passed in April 2013, and in May 2013 my fiancé's father passed from cancer. And the list goes on . . .

Every experience has taught me to dig and go deeper within myself, often times for self-preservation and holding onto God. Prayer, meditation, exercise, music and being out in nature are what have held my hand and helped me to exhale my pain. Yet I know I've had these hard times to be strong enough to continue the journey.

Building my business has taken years of sacrifice, sheer determination, perseverance, hard work and a strong vision. Yet my work is more than a job, it's my vocation. I'm simply here to serve humanity. I have created an empire, and now like the phoenix rising from the ashes, so is my business. I set up my own radio station, Qarma Broadcast. I also have my own therapy based business and my own intuitive psychic line with a difference. I am a gifted Intuitive Healer and work with clients on a deep intuitive level working on their emotional, physical, spiritual and psychological issues; it's beautiful to see peoples' lives transformed within a very short space of time; hence why I am known as "**The 60 Second Soul Liberator.**"

Yet I am much more than who I have described above. As I learn more about me, I expand into a limitless potpourri of the abundance of life and into the opening up of more of my gifts and the fundamental essence of who I am. I am the chameleon of my own life's story. As I have grown I have seen different people at different points in time, discovering at each stage a different aspect of who I am. For me the University of Life is not in achieving a piece of paper, but in achieving mastery of the self, walking and talking my truth. For the first time in my life I have manifested the most amazing love, friendship and bond with a significant other, my soul mate and fiancé, but I had to learn first to step into my truth and love and honour myself.

Therefore, wherever you are in your life, whatever you have experienced, find that place in your heart to **know** that your pain can be transformed and healed. You don't need to carry it all your life. Use pain as your stepping stone for greater things. When the tough gets going and the going gets tough, look up, reach out, cry out and God will hear you. Surround yourself with positive people. Take away any judgment from yourself because it makes it easier for you to face your mirror of truth so that you can move forward to deal with life. Negativity, resentment, gossip and hatred will keep you bound. Remember, you have all the answers within you, and until you forgive yourself and learn to love yourself, no one else will.

Joy Ibibo

Joy Ibibo was born in the city Port Harcourt, Rivers State, Nigeria. She attended GGSS Harbour Road for high school and Rivers State Polytechnic where she obtained a degree in Accounting.

She has worked with Nigerian Agip Oil Company, Leadway Assurance Company and CIMEC Petrocorr, and presently runs a catering and event management business. She is also an online network marketer. She lives in Port Harcourt.

+2348182207454
jocyng,ojpee@gmail.com

Chapter 6
Personal Accountability

By Joy Ibibo

Having been through many experiences in life—some good, some not so good, some exceptional and some really bad—I can only remain thankful for the love of God. There is something about the love of God that gives us courage and confidence to face life with boldness, openness and honesty. It enables us to live our lives authentically; we don't have to pretend to be somebody else, because we are secure in ourselves.

Now and again, I take stock of my life and reflect on what's happening in and around me and my business. It's important because, I realize in the process how I am, and am motivated to count my blessings and even name them one by one.

My journey in life is really a testimony of God's goodness, because when I look back at where and how I started, all I can see is a strong woman who is confident in the ability of God, and is making it against all odds.

I started my business when my mates were still collecting pocket money from their parents. My first capital was my school fees. I was already in college when my dad lost his job, and responsibility for the family rested solely on my mum. Things were tough; sometimes we didn't even know where the next meal would be coming from. So when my mates were busy thinking of parties and boyfriends, I was thinking of how to make money

It wasn't easy because I had no experience, no substantial capital and no advice whatsoever. I was just a young girl with a passion to use whatever hobby or talent I could to earn a living. At that point surviving was of utmost importance, so there were no plans to sustain the growth of the business. In the past, I was always making curtains, bed sheets, duvets and also cooking for friends and family, but it was absolutely for free. When I decided to turn my hobby into a business, people had to get used to it because it wasn't free anymore!

My business did not start booming overnight. I lost most of the money because of some bad decisions. I sold most of my goods on credit and people did not pay. I felt I was up against something stronger than myself. At that point I was bitter and angry with my family, my friends and myself. I felt I was cursed. Help was not forthcoming from anywhere, and I almost dropped out of school.

Sometimes in life we are faced with such a challenge that it looks like the whole world is against us and giving up may seem like the only option we have. In fact, giving up becomes the easy way out; but if we take a moment to look inside of ourselves, we will find the answers that we seek.

I almost gave up on myself; I was confused and in pain. My friends and even some relatives made fun of me and scorned me, secretly and openly, whenever I asked them for help. I was told that I would amount to no good because my parents will never be able to give my siblings and me a good life. The turning point in my life was when I became homeless.

Before then, I was used to blaming everyone but myself for why my life was not working out the way I wanted. Becoming homeless was an eye opener. I knew I had to take action in the right direction.

I realized assigning blame would do me no good. I needed to change a lot of things about myself. First, I had a serious conversation with myself. I brought out my mirror (full length) and talked to myself. I said to myself, "Joy, you are a beautiful lady. You are wonderfully and fearfully made by God. You are the pride of God and He loves you so much. You have so much to give to your world, so don't let anybody talk you down or accept anything less than who you are, because you are a wonder." I did this constantly—when I was in the bathroom, in the kitchen, you name it. I stopped feeling sorry for myself and wishing things were different.

There is something a lot of persons are not aware of; they believe and act like God owes them something or has to change their situation. The truth is God has done everything He needs to do for everybody to live a beautiful life, but the desire and choice to live that beautiful life lies with us. The change we desire lies with us. As I am sure you are aware, no change is easy or comes without effort. Personal change cannot be accomplished by technology; it requires commitment, persistence, determination and, above all, patience.

When I decided my life needed a change, it was a decision nobody took for me. I knew I had to start taking 100% responsibility for my life. I took responsibility for my actions and decisions, and I became accountable for my responsibilities and my goals. I had to understand that it was up to me to make sure I am doing what I know I should be doing. This changed my life so much!

While in school I got a job in an oil-servicing firm as an industrial trainee (IT), so I had to combine work, school and business. School now had to be on a part time basis. For my business, I had to get some basic training, it was not enough that I love to cook or decorate. I attended seminars and workshops to enhance what I love doing. My business picked up; although I started with zero capital, I learned to start small and grow.

Knowing that I was responsible for the growth of my business, I told everybody I came in touch with and handed out business cards and flyers. Before long I was getting responses from people. Although I still do some jobs for free, I always get referrals for doing so. As my business grew, I had to resign from my job to focus on it full time.

Today I am a graduate, I run a successful event management business, together with the interior décor aspect, and I also earn a good income online. I thank my aunt a great deal for giving me the talk of my life, because if she had not done so, I probably would still be living in her house and at her mercy. I hold myself accountable for everything that goes on in my life; nobody dictates if I should be happy or not.

My parents may not have given me the kind of life they wanted, but I created the life I wanted. I may not be where I want to be yet, but certainly I am not where I used to be. My dad passed away a few years ago from a stroke. I am sure if he could see me, he would be beaming with smiles.

This is why I can boldly say God has been so good to me, because He has made my life really beautiful. What I have or don't have doesn't't matter anymore; I learn to draw strength from God. I don't focus on my weaknesses, but in the strength God has given to me. It's not like I don't have or face challenges; I just know that tough times will not always last.

So when I look in the mirror, I no longer see that girl with low self-confidence who lives in fear and thinks she is a failure. All I can see now is a confident woman who is full of life, and does not pretend to be anybody else because she knows she can be more and refuses to live in fear because she is loved.

Someone wrote somewhere, "Whether you are 15 or 60 years old, let today be the day you make the commitment to yourself that you will never again require anyone else to hold you accountable." Holding yourself accountable is nothing more than following through with your commitments and responsibilities. It is doing what you know you should do, when you should do it. You must make a choice to take a chance or your life will never change. When life throws lemons at you, you learn to make lemonade.

Take control! This is your life, so you have to be responsible for it, nobody will do it for you.

Kim Schuld

Kim Schuld is the coach who can get you out of a rut, around a detour, or charting your route for a completely new destination in top-speed time.

A key to Kim's approach lies in helping her clients find their starting point and using it to create a clear path to the next destination without getting lost or distracted along the way. She uses the timeless principles of personality assessments, goal setting and success pillars to help you find your true life purpose and follow it.

Kim splits her time between Fort Worth, Texas and international travel.

www.thelifejourneycoach.com
www.dumpdieting.com
kim@thelifejourneycoach.com
LifeJourneyCoach kimschuld

Chapter 7
Letting Go Of The Cookies

By Kim Schuld

I t was the best relationship of my life.

    This time I was the one calling the shots. I was getting exactly what I wanted without complaint or pushback for the first time in my life. There were no demands to do things I didn't't want to do. There were no expectations to be a good little girl, or the perfect looking arm candy for a man.

This relationship was safe. I had created it from the beginning to be what I wanted, what I *needed* it to be. After years of emotional and verbal abuse, I had created my safe haven.

It was killing me. I was in a relationship that was robbing me of my physical life as it was shutting down my emotional life.

I was in a relationship with food. It was sweet when I wanted sweet. It was salty when I wanted salty. It was creamy when I wanted creamy and crunchy when I wanted crunchy. I had no complaints about my new lover until I had to shop for new clothes; and even then there were people and places willing to accommodate my new lover and me.

As my body was increasing in girth, I was encouraged to admit that I needed to shop in the "big girls" department. For many women, that might have been a wakeup call. For me, the shock was not enough to prevent me from calling up Pizza Hut every Friday night. Inside this new world of plus-sized clothing, I found nurturing women who were more than happy to see me join their ranks. They liked me. They were kind to me. They were not the ones to intervene and shake me into awareness that I was in another abusive relationship. I certainly Wasn't going to admit that to myself because I was still nursing the wounds from the last abusive relationship, and the food was my balm.

This new relationship with food began after a very challenging time of my life.

I don't know where I found the courage to leave—but I did. One fateful night my eyes were opened to the facts that I had been maligned, yelled at, made fun of, chastised, criticized and manipulated by a man who I finally realized would never accept me. He said the words "I love you" at least fifteen times a day, but the fact of the matter was, he didn't't even like me. For him, I was never going to be thin enough, pretty enough and thereby good enough. The day I left him I weighed less than I had since high school, but I was miserable, unhealthy, and ill equipped to sort through the emotional wreckage.

Five years later, I had gained one hundred pounds and was on several medications for obesity-related conditions and depression. I was desperate to be loved, desperate to have children; I hated who I was and what I had become. I certainly wasn't attracting any husband prospects this way, but I wasn't ready to give up on life yet. I needed to make a major change.

I decided that this was it. I was going to take control of my life and lose weight. I hired a personal trainer to put together a daily plan for me, to hold me accountable and to kick my butt. I changed all of my eating habits and became the calorie Nazi of the family gatherings. In seven months I lost 86 pounds and was looking pretty darn good. My trainer assured me that when the weight came off I would have all the desires of my heart, including a new man.

As all the girls in Texas do, I highlighted my long hair with blonde, put on the cute clothes and strutted around in my high heels exuding my essence. And still, no man would come within one hundred feet of me.

I used online dating. I asked men on dates and hung out at sports bars chatting with men endlessly about their stupid fishing competitions and still, *nothing.*

I just *knew* it was because I wasn't slim enough yet. So instead of just attending classes at the gym, I ramped up the activity and became an instructor. I was at several locations teaching anywhere from six to fifteen classes each week. I was back down to my college weight. I told everyone I was single and available and looking. And the dating calendar was bare.

I had done all this work, and didn't't get the result I was expecting. I had abandoned my favourite foods, denied myself pleasure, given my schedule over to the gym and still, there was no one. What in the world was I doing this for?

The missing key was this: I hadn't made any of these changes out of love and appreciation for the fearfully and wonderfully made body God had entrusted to me. I had bought into the myth that thin equalled love, and that only thin women deserved love.

I also had never been taught how to handle negative emotions. During my childhood, anger was not allowed. I didn't't know how to express my true emotions in a healthy way. As I unravelled the damage of my failed relationship, I was forced to examine those childhood patterns and to feel things that I had no strategy to navigate. So I ate. I was afraid that feeling anger, disappointment, fear, or pain in any form would drown me, so I clung to the life raft of pizza and later, obsessive exercise.

It wasn't until I worked as hard on the inside as I had on the outside that I could release the remnants of anger, disappointment and sadness over my failed relationship and lost childhood. Facing my emotional eating demons freed me from the pursuit of pretty and allowed me to start the pursuit of empowered.

To break my emotional food addiction, I had to learn to feel my true emotions; raw, unfiltered and without cookies. My self-loathing didn't start with that guy. He was simply a manifestation of the beliefs I'd already held about myself. As long as I was afraid to feel my true emotions, the gremlins were running the show. As I learned to let those negative feelings have their say and then to release them, I was slowly releasing the grip food had over me. Eventually, I came to a place of balance and self-love. That included acceptance that I might never have a husband or children.

Some of the weight came back, but it does not define me. I continue to work out and maintain a healthy meal plan as a lifestyle, but I no longer spend hours at the gym and don't paste pictures of fitness models on my refrigerator. In my new life, I exercise to feel strong and to feel comfortable in my clothes. I choose foods to boost my energy and improve my brain function. I used to coach people at the gym through teaching classes and personal training. Now I coach them to face their relationship with food to find the hidden hurts and to heal old wounds in order to release weight.

Here are my top 5 tips for starting your own process to change your relationship with food:

1. **Keep a food journal**. Note everything you eat, the amount, where you ate it, what led you to eat at that time, and what you were feeling. You need to map your emotional connections to food in order to break those connections.
2. **Be courageous and name your true feelings**. Many of us say that we eat when we are bored or stressed. Those are not feelings, they are conditions. Speak your true feelings: I am disappointed in my marriage. I am lonely. I am afraid of success. I am angry at my father.
3. **View food as fuel**, not as your best friend or as something to be feared. We have to fuel our bodies, so there's no going "cold turkey."
4. **Change your mindset** from "dieting as punishment" to "eating for life." Food should be satisfying and nutritious, not covering pain. I trust that you will know the difference.
5. **Exercise every day,** hard enough to raise your heart rate. The endorphins created by activity will free your brain from the grip of food worries.

Breaking my food addiction brought joy and ease into my life. I never could have known how to freely and genuinely love myself without changing my strategy for handling negative emotions. Being able to do it without food has saved my life.

Nguavese M. Aminu

❧

Nguavese M. Aminu is the third of six children from Benue State, Nigeria. She is married and is blessed with two lovely boys. She is an entrepreneur with a catering business and also engaged in international education marketing. She is the founder and co-owner of Lushatshe Services Limited. She has been running her business for three years now. She has a Bachelor 's degree in chemistry from the University of Jos-Plateau state, and has 8 years working experience in administration. Before concentrating fully on her business, she worked for a student recruiting agency, a radio station and a non-profit organization, all based in Port Harcourt, Rivers State, Nigeria.

nguavese.aminu nguavese1@yahoo.com
facebook.com/namokaha
@nguavese

Chapter 8
You Are Your Own Cheerleader

By Nguavese M. Aminu

"The world will beat you down sometimes, but it is in your hands to hold yourself up always. When you decide to follow the world to beat yourself down, either by accepting what or who they describe you to be, then are you truly DEFEATED."

I have lived all my life making and choosing my path with little or no guidance. I can say this: It has been really difficult! There were many times when I felt confused and insecure. Responsibility was second nature to me. I took care of myself and my younger brothers from a young age. This got me thinking, "Why do I have to do all these chores?" then I realized it was because my mother, who was a nurse at the time, needed extra support. I burdened myself with trying to be a support system for my mother, my siblings and myself. With finances low, six children to take care of as well as dependant relatives, hiring domestic assistance was not an option.

Considering the state of our home, I decided to work harder in order to create a better future for myself and, definitely did not want to be put through such stress when I had my home and children.

I left home for secondary school, more determined than ever to work hard and be the best I could at everything I did. I would become a doctor someday and make a lot of money to support everyone. I thought not only is the profession a prestigious one, it would allow me to earn a lot of money. I was wrong. I worked hard through my first and second junior years but life became harder at home and, of course, it affected me in many more ways than I can put on paper.

I completed my secondary education in good time and my leadership nature earned me a place as a prefect. I knew that come what may, if I stayed responsible and keep working hard, I would eventually succeed because I have a positive staying power.

When I got to university I knew that my profession of choice was eluding me. In that moment, I decided I would rather be a business tycoon than a doctor who works for a salary. Now; how does someone studying chemistry at the university move to studying business? This was a real dilemma. However, the best decision was to continue the path until when an opportunity to gain practical skills to run a business comes my way in the future.

Thankfully, I found a job as a waitress in a café during my third year. With the university educational sector in my country striking regularly, I took this to be another way to gainfully spend that time away from the classroom whilst learning how to run a business. The job continued on a part-time basis even after the strike was called off.

It was sometimes awkward to see my mates come into the café to grab a bite and I had to serve them. Some would say; "You should not be doing this" (implying that the work was demeaning). It was at this café that I learned to save, be accountable, customer service, etc. I like to call it 'the core business skills that are not taught in the four walls of a classroom or boardroom'.

After university, a great job opportunity to work at the British student recruitment agency came my way. It was a good feeling to learn the skills needed for the job. I worked there for a couple of years as a Counsellor, Recruitment Officer then a Recruitment Manager—it was a beautiful experience to climb up the ladder of leadership and get paid for it too.

During this time I registered a business and started to supply toiletries to hotels and restaurants. Basically, I juggled work, my supply business and being a mother and a wife. I had to keep up with deadlines and targets at work and sometimes I was late with supplies for my clients. Other times the clients would not pay for previous supplies and then request new ones. I had my capital and profit all tied up, so I had to source funds to meet these supply requests, because if I didn't't then I would not be considered a serious businesswoman.

It was hard, to say the least. There were many times I could not balance my accounts, but I refused to be discouraged. I needed to keep my job as the business was not financially stable. Coupled with that there were a lot of politics at my job which I tried not to be a part of, as I recognised that you will attract opposition if you decide to rise above other's expectations of you. To get through that time I reminded myself of my vision.

One day, I went to work only to be informed in the late afternoon that I was being relieved of my role for not meeting targets. It was most unexpected and traumatizing experience since I had been in this role for only seven months. I gave myself one month to grieve and think strategically on how to move forward. I had not saved enough to survive without a steady income neither did I attain enough business management skills to run a viable business. I recognised I had to quickly learn how to make the business profitable. As a result, I taught myself using webinars, information materials and attended self-discovery/business seminars whenever I could. It was strenuous. I did not want the little I had saved to dwindle without securing a consistent source of income.

In a bid to stay relevant, I started a Multi Level Marketing (MLM) business because I saw it as a platform to make money and find fulfilment. This is when my moment of realisation hit me. I thought, "You are doing all this marketing for another company whilst yours is dying from no high level marketing." EUREKA! BINGO! BRAVO! A veil just dropped from my eyes and a light bulb came alive. You cannot believe the rush of fresh energy into my system.

All these ideas just came to me. One of the ideas was to find partner institutions that my company can represent so that the skills I have acquired over the years at the student recruitment agency will be put in full use and create wealth for me and my family.

However, this time I will be getting all the benefits that comes with the effort that I have put in. Then I can give yourself a treat each time I accomplish a target, because there will be lots of them. The second idea was; I love cooking and I can get people to pay me to cook for them. Partner with a friend who will be there when I have too much on my plate. Three, find a leisure activity that I enjoy doing and offer it for a fee to friends and family.

The company could branch out to do anything at all. It was amazing! So let's start with the first idea. I did get a partnership to represent a group of schools. With the partnership papers signed, I swung into multi-tasking. I was involved in marketing, administration, accounting and customer service, not to mention being a mother and wife. Marketing was easy, but getting people to commit financially was cumbersome. I needed that commitment from my clients.

Slowly but surely I got clients and was in business. I did not have an office, so I worked from home. Some clients were not convinced I was legitimate, so they could not commit financially. I had to get a job to support my business logistics. I got one with a radio station where I worked for about a year. I was on the road for three hours every day, which took a toll on me mentally and physically. So I resigned from that position.

I was so afraid of not working, because what I earned as a salary kept the business afloat. So I found an NGO closer to home and started the grind again. Then I got pregnant with my second child, but went back to work when my son was two months old. This was so difficult that I could not deal; however, I also wanted the business to be self-funded.

Faced with this dilemma, my husband came to the rescue. He secured funds for the business. I was so excited because I had been self-funded for so long. He must have seen that I am no quitter! This came as a much-needed relief, so I resigned my position at the NGO to take care of the things most important to me—my family and my business. I have achieved more success at my business now than ever before because all my energy and creativity is 100% in it. I am not where I envisioned being, but I am well on my way.

My advice is: Fear is a deterrent. Perseverance will always give birth to help and success. Stay with your vision. If you see it in your mind, you can and will achieve it. Cheer yourself on, because nobody will do that for you.

I am indeed my own cheerleader.

Olutope Lawal

My name is Olutope Lawal, but most people call me Topsy or Tope. I am a single mother of three and a woman of purpose, passion, poise and vision with a mission to have a positive impact on the lives of those I encounter. I believe we are created for a divine purpose; we need to find that purpose and live to the fullest by using our talent and potential to better others and ourselves. I believe in kindness, love and positive energy, which is why I named my foundation NIYILOLA FOUNDATION meaning this is where the wealth is! The wealth is within us; it's inside of us. I am a woman that believes in God and his creation. I am a child of God. I believe in Jesus Christ and through Him I received my salvation and freedom to think. He is the source of my strength. I am a philanthropist and a philosopher. I believe in leaving a positive legacy for generations to come through my wisdom, lifestyle, love and kindness. I am also an event planner, event manager, humanitarian worker and advocate for human rights and uniting families in crisis, and against domestic and child abuse. I also co-founded the Nigerian Events Awards UK (NEA-UK).

07417570759
Topsy161 divineinspiration15@gmail.com
niyilolafoundation@gmail.com
Niyilola Foundation DivineInspiration1Events

Chapter 9
Joy of Living

By Olutope Lawal

Whatever you are and whoever you are, always strive to be yourself because God did not create us to be intimidated by others. God created us to be in harmony with one another. So if you are surrounded by people who are higher than you, be happy for them and strive to get to your own destination, not someone else's destination. We all have unique qualities, so look for what makes you special. Do not become like a zombie who doesn't't know its part and copies other people. It's good to have a role model or people whose lifestyle you admire, but don't become so engrossed in the act of becoming someone else.

The time we live in is so full of dos and don'ts, such as "don't eat this, don't do that." We have become so engrossed in celebrity lifestyles, becoming rich quickly and using the latest technology that we often forget the purpose and meaning of life. Our generation is so used to buying the best shoes and bags or the latest gadgets that we end up becoming so vain that we don't realize that this is vanity upon vanity.

If you go to party these days and are not wearing the latest bling, you are not reckon with but one thing I always say is that many of these people, if you look into their lives, you will realize that there is something missing spiritually, physically or emotionally, which is why they use material wealth to cover up their shortcomings.

This is not the case for everybody, but if you look around you these days, there are many reasons to question a lot of things happening around us.

To be clear, it's good to be successful, but the most successful people don't need to display their wealth and oppress others because of their wealth.

Sometimes being wealthy is not seen through the material things, rather it is the amount of people you impact and whose lives you touch with your words of encouragement, your kindness, your prayers and your love.

Yes, money is good, but what you do with your money is what matters at the end of the day.

I may not like to wear what everybody is wearing, but that does not make me less of a human, nor does it mean I am poor. It means that I am unique, that I love to create my own trends. There is joy in living when you love yourself and who you are without anyone making you feel less of a human. You don't have to copy other people. If you do not make your own decisions in life, other people will make them for you.

I want my message to be clear: be yourself. Let God be your centre of attention, love people around you and don't try to impress anyone. If people truly love you, then they will accept you with your shortcomings. If you always have to impress them, then they don't truly appreciate you or love you for the person God created you to be. You need to think twice about these kinds of people who always expect you to follow their thinking or instruction. It's good for people to give advice sometimes, but when it becomes a habit you need to go back on your knees for God to direct and lead you.

I believe everyone has a choice in this life, and our choices and decisions always lead us to wherever we find ourselves—whether it's good or bad.

Always strive to be yourself and remember that there is a reason why you are here reading this book now; so ask yourself, "What is my purpose? What am I here for? What do I love to do? Where do I love to be? Who inspires me? What is my personal goal in life?" Write all your answers down on a sheet of paper and stick it on the wall to always remember what you want to do. You might come up with loads of inspirations or

ideas of what you want to do or become. Out of all the ideas, whichever one is strong and gives you sleepless nights is your purpose. Write that down and figure out how you will achieve your goals. Visualize what it will mean to you once you achieve this goal or purpose. Once you can visualize this aspiration, break it down into sections to figure out specific steps and where you may need help.

Whatever your purpose, remember that starting will not be easy. You might be scared to take that risk, or you may feel so comfortable that you don't want to shake things up. Keep yourself motivated by constantly reminding yourself of the end goal. Imagine yourself on the podium to greatness with your friends and family there to celebrate your success! What are you waiting for? Take that scary step to achieve your purpose. Your family for generations to come will thank you for that.

When your life is going smoothly and everything is going well for you, thank God for it, and never rely on it or oppress anyone with it because no condition is ever permanent. If your life is not going according to your own plan or wish, don't allow your situation to make you forget God or start feeling like the victim. Seek the face of God, who will connect you with divine helpers. Check yourself; what can you do differently? In everything remember to always give God the glory, both good and bad. Everything works out for our own good if only we can just wait on the Lord. It can be tough, but if you just have faith God will never leave you.

God always shows up in a situation that everyone has condemned. The Lord always makes a way when you least expect it. Do you know that you are only living on half-baked bread if you are not improving on yourself? We can never stop learning. You alone can stop yourself from living a purposeful life. The more you start to feel great within, the more you will discover that you deserve greatness. Empty yourself of pride and everything you hang on to and start to live a fulfilled life. What you think is important in life is not necessarily the most important. Allow God to show you the path to an abundant and fulfilling life. Change your view and vision about life and everything will start to change. Seek the spirituality and strength within yourself. As for me, I am on the road to discovery, but at least I have learned that whatever I put my mind to I can achieve.

Petrina Kamara

Petrina Kamara is the CEO/Creative Designer of Petiz Fashions Ltd. and the founder of Petiz Fashion Accessories. Her brand is about happiness, confidence, uniqueness and empowerment. Growing up, she had always considered her image, appearance, character and reputation her main brands.

Petrina is known for her inner strength and resilience to life's challenges. She is a survivor who is loyal but her no nonsense approach to life has made her a controversial character in her community. She is driven, creative, innovative, talented, very intelligent, a fantastic mum, has an excellent sense of humor and she has a personality and presence that lights up a room. Petrina's underprivileged upbringing has kept her well grounded, very focused and drawn her to charities relating to her life experiences. Most importantly, she has always been proud of her background and achievements. She sees herself as a consistent work in progress who believes only mediocrity can be trusted to always be at its best.

www.petizonline.com or **www.petizfashions.co.uk.**
petizfashions@hotmail.co.uk
facebook.com/petizfashionaccessories.
twitter.com/petizfashions Petizfashionaccessories

Chapter 10
How My Situation Became My Motivation

By Petrina Kamara

I t was cold winter morning, three days after Christmas in 1998 and we were still celebrating. My Aunty Jo and late Uncle Tieh had travelled from Manchester to stay with me until the baby arrived. I went through the excruciating pain but that evening my Adrian was born weighing 7lbs 11oz. Adrian had always been my favorite boy name, and from this moment on, my life really began.

I was a single parent by choice. I wanted to carry on with my pregnancy because at 26 years old this was my very first pregnancy. I was very surprised to be pregnant in the first place because a few years prior, I was diagnosed with Polycystic Ovary Syndrome and told my chances of getting pregnant were slim. This news was distressing, but after two years of medication and treatments Adrian was conceived.

Adrian's dad's absence left a big void in our lives. It reminded me of my dad who left me in Sierra Leone in 1973 when I was only a year old, to study law in the US. He is now a lecturer and lawyer in Baltimore, but I do not have a relationship with him. The last time I physically saw him was when he came on vacation in 1979. He suddenly stopped calling and supporting me when I was 13 years old. Life became a struggle, but I was awarded a scholarship by Plan International to support my education. I was naturally academically inclined, but at the time there were not enough funds to see me through university; that too was a privilege we could not afford.

I was raised by my two grand aunties in a home that lacked many things; however, being their first grandchild I was pampered. My grandparents used to call me "Petpet," and people in my neighbourhood often thought I was spoiled because of that nickname. Until I left Sierra Leone at age 21, I had never done my own laundry or even cooked a meal. I was raised to be proud of who I was and be content with what I had—two values that have shaped me into the woman I am today. I practically grew up in a household where electricity was a privilege, yet I brought home excellent results. Sitting in private cars was an absolute luxury, but it never bothered me seeing fellow schoolmates have it all. I stayed focused and content because I had something most of them didn't have—a stable and loving home built with zinc where I was treated like a princess. By the time I had Adrian, I was determined that my children would not lack anything.

As a beautiful young girl, growing up in one of the roughest parts of Freetown, I had a choice which direction to take my life. Allow older rich men to violate me in exchange for privileges or be content with what I had and focus on my education and becoming a better woman. I remained focused, however, one of my greatest emotional setbacks was a horrific sexual attack I encountered a year before coming to the UK. It was a random attack by four men right in front of my boyfriend at the time who was badly beaten and restrained. I was devastated. I was ashamed I had been violated by people I may never be able to identify, but it was from this experience that I developed an absolute intolerance for certain types of men, an instant allergy to playboys and controlling men who displayed no respect for women.

I was raised by two strong, illiterate women who upheld respect in our Liberian-Sierra Leonean community. They were both sisters to my maternal grandmother who passed away when I was only seven. Success in Africa is generally based on who your parents are, or, as a woman, how much of your body and soul you are willing to give up. Parents of rich kids elevate their children by calling in favours from their equally powerful friends or spending enough to give them the best education. Either way, I stood no chance, so I decided to create my own opportunities. It was that one-man journey that got me this far. It is my principle that no matter how powerful or privileged anyone is, if they do not show me respect, I will not associate with them. I worked hard to be independent, so I cannot be humiliated for money or favours. Today, I'm am proudly raising two kids who are aware of the importance of education and good behaviour, just as I was raised. I am a proud mummy.

I was a happy child being raised underprivileged, but what I lacked in material things I got richly in the love and honour my grandparents passed on to me. I was never a demanding child, so whatever I wanted my grandparents would provide; on a few occasions they sold their few prized personal possessions just to provide for me. They were proud I was doing so well at school. I was raised like a princess. My mum, commonly known as Miss Joko, was married to my sister's dad, so she lived for 18 years in a town outside Freetown called Kabala and she sponsored the entire family. I was raised never to succumb to problems or hardships, to be very independent, be a lady, love everyone, be open and honest about my feelings and always stand up or fight for what I believed in. These values helped me through the next chapters in my life.

I got married in 2007 and had my daughter Farrina in 2008, ten years after I had my son Adrian. I filed for divorce in late 2009, which was very difficult. I wanted a loving and stable marriage so that my children could have the conventional family life I never had. In late 2010 my son was diagnosed with Autistic spectrum disorder after years of assessments, speech problems and learning difficulties. After my divorce, I looked for ways to redirect my energy, something I could do on a daily basis to take away the pain and betrayal I felt from my short-lived marriage. Then I got the idea to make jewellery and subsequently, my successful line of accessories.

My idea to customize accessories started when I was in secondary school. I was drawn to needlework, designing and arts and crafts. I remember many of my schoolmates used to buy and wear the same plain shoes from the same vendors. I did not like them, but had no choice, so I started customizing my shoes with lace and buttons to look different. In 2013, my hobby of customizing and making accessories became an established business. In 2011, I received a special recognition award from the Global Women Inventors and Innovators Network for my creative skills. In September, I was nominated in the best Female Designer category at Black Entertainment Film Fashion TV Awards. In November 2013, my company won an award as the Best New Business at the Sierra Leone Excellence Awards. I was fired up!

2013 came with some brutal challenges. I started the year with a spinal injury that I sustained while moving. As a result, I lost sensation on and off in my right arm and fingers. I was told that I needed a serious operation on my neck to fix it. I am right hand dominant and I work full time, so the question that came to my mind was, "what do you do when the very essence of you is under threat?" I am a crafts woman and an accessories designer; therefore my hands are essential to my work. By mid-2013 I experienced betrayal and deep-rooted jealousy from people who I trusted with my children's lives. With all these experiences, it was now time to redirect my energy and reinvest in my business. I was not angry, I was resilient and this was going to be a major turning point in my life. My strongest conviction is that God wanted me to come out of these situations unscathed and a stronger woman in preparation for a brighter future.

Let's go back to advice I received from a former boss, "Petrina, in order to be the best at whatever you do and survive it, you have to be thick skinned." The next chapters in my life did not have any room for leeches or moles; I needed a clean break, so I started associating with positive and productive people. Here is my daily recital from a personal development program: "my future is in my hands. I know that change is possible and only I can bring about the necessary changes."

I also live by this quote from George Eliot, "it is never too late to be what you might have been." Interpreted, you are NEVER too old to pursue your dreams; therefore, at age 39 I began my business journey. Nothing else mattered at this point, because as Walt Disney once said, "All dreams can come true if we have the courage to pursue them." I am committed and in pursuit of the ultimate fulfilment with a thick skin. I cannot be affected and will not be infected by anyone or anything. I keep my work in perspective because I'm a work in progress. This is how my past became my motivation, and I hope you can learn from this.

Rosemary Pharo

Rosemary Pharo lives in South London with her husband and two teenage children. She helps people become happier, healthier and more successful using a creative approach and range of techniques from Reiki, massage, meta-aromatherapy and Psych-K®. She teaches Reiki to people of all ages and is a student of Reiki Kyokai. She runs creative self-development workshops, and is a fully trained antenatal teacher offering holistic birth preparation using Reiki.

www.RosemaryKpharo.net
info@rosemarykpharo.net
@babyreikiclass
linkedin.com/pub/rosemary-pharo/16/645/215

Chapter 11
Love At First Life

By Rosemary Pharo

A few days ago I was sitting in a café with an old school friend. Our kids are the same age, and we found ourselves sharing the same thought.

We care for others the whole time, but who cares for us? Who is there to look after us?

And isn't't this what women all over the world find? We are carers and confidantes. We give and we look after. We are strong, but we often don't realize our strength.

My life had begun in the West Midlands, north of Birmingham, where I spent my first ten years with my parents and my younger brothers. Walsall Wood is an old, ex-mining village just outside the leather capital that was Walsall. We lived in a three story huge blue brick Victorian vicarage. One extremity had rising damp and the other, dry rot. Once it was knocked down we moved next door to a modern purpose-built house. As a vicarage next door to a Church we attracted our fair share of the disturbed and destitute. There was the axe-wielding maniac who tried to break in because he claimed he was St John and we'd stolen his church. Then there was the lady who came in and took all her clothes off.

South East London, where we moved, was a very different environment. People in the Midlands can be pretty blunt and open. People in South East London tend to be much more reserved. It was a true culture shock.

In the Midlands I had spent much time riding my bike, climbing up on the creaky roof of the old cricket pavilion in a corner of the large garden and playing with cap guns and bows aand arrows. From having family just down the road, we went there being no family around.

As a child I loved singing and was very creative. My London secondary school, girls only selective, was mind numbingly deadly in its focus and its staff's apparent narrow-mindedness. I thought of it as a kind of academic sausage factory. The only thing that mattered there were the grades the girls got. There weren't't many laughs. As individuals, we didn't't seem to matter. Or at least that is how it seemed. Now I feel even more that especially with the messages from TV and media, that what we need to nurture in ourselves and in our children is a sense of who we really are, to trust our inner instincts and to have a good laugh at what life throws at us.

Back then, having been spat out of the other end of the conveyor belt, I went to college, got a degree and somehow fell into copywriting as a profession. The deadline-oriented atmosphere of the ad agency suited me. It made some use of my creativity. And because it was recruitment, there was some focus on people's desires and hopes and, of course, I liked the adrenaline and buzz, because that was what I knew best. That was my default setting, if you like.

However, was I being true to myself? I don't think so. Was I really happy? No, not truly. I muddled along like most of us do, habitually anaesthetizing the inner disquiet and questioning.

Life, however, had decided things were becoming way too comfortable and started to play hardball. It was 1993 and I was recovering from a foot operation that I had put off for years. Sometime in my teens, a piece of bone had just died in my foot. There had been low-level constant pain, but I simply blocked it out, kept my shoes done up tight and carried on doing whatever I chose to. No way was I going to listen to my body. Rather than enquire into the cause of the pain, I'd simply blocked it out and kept going. Finally though, I had found a surgeon who I trusted, and submitted to surgery under local anaesthetics. It was the right time.

While I was recuperating, I had a phone call from my employer who said that due to the recession there was no longer a job for me, and by the way, could they have my car back too, please? Almost at the same time, my then relationship came to an end.

It seemed that I had lost my job, my car; my relationship and my home in one go. Just about everything that gives people some meaning in life had been taken away in one fell swoop.

It was a big, big, shock. Enough to have me contemplating whether it was worth carrying on. But it took this big shock to propel me into a state of self-inquiry that I had not previously entered. And so I thank all those involved in this shock for playing their part in moving me forward. The worst things that happen often give us the most opportunity for growth.

I took the first step to reconnecting with my real self by playing a taped old horoscope reading. It had been something fun at work, created by one of my colleague's mum years earlier. I hadn't taken it very seriously, and it had been slung somewhere in a drawer. But, by playing it, I finally sat down and asked myself what was the point of my life? What was I here to do?

And I got an answer; Loud and clear.

It was to be four more years until I really started to move forward. Getting married and having my first child happened first, and then I finally started studying. I knew I had to work within the field of healing, and I began with a course that combined classical bodywork with essential oils, counselling, art therapy approaches, trauma release protocols and working with energy.

I wasn't comfortable with the energy technique taught in the course. It felt too open. But one of my fellow students kept repeating that "this was a bit like Reiki," which she had studied in the US. There was something about Reiki that drew me in. I knew nothing about it except that it felt like surrendering.

Metaphorically throwing my arms in the air, I opened the Yellow Pages and found an entry for Reiki just down the road. Nervously ringing up, a warm voice informed me that there was a seminar the next week. "I'll be there," I said.

And that was the beginning of feeling that I was coming home to me.

In the past 15 years I've studied a number of different approaches to Reiki and added Psych-K®, which opened up the understanding of the effect of subconscious beliefs on the life we live. I've taught Reiki and been involved in drawing up national standards for the professional practice of Reiki in the UK.

Every day when I practice Reiki on myself, I come closer to who I am. I feel close to universal love and compassion. When I need to, I also am not afraid to face my inner demons, walk into inner pockets of darkness and understand what I need to learn and heal within myself.

I also found I was drawn strongly to work with pregnancy and childbirth. So in addition to my wide range of clients, I studied with the UK's largest charity to gain a university-level diploma in antenatal education. I ended up running classes for over 1,000 parents-to-be and continue to gain a breadth of knowledge of what parents feel, need and want.

But in my heart of hearts I know that for a meaningful change to be made in the future lives of children and the adults they become, women must have as calm and loving a pregnancy as possible, free from as many worries as possible. This is evident in the fact that the research is clear that the environment that children experience in the womb has a long-term effect on their mental, emotional and physical well-being.

So what we need are programmes that support and value pregnant women from the beginning of pregnancy; programmes that invest in future lives by investing in the emotional well-being of pregnant women and their families. Some would even say that this starts before pregnancy—clearing limiting beliefs and emotional baggage and gaining a good understanding of what to eat and what not to eat.

This is why I have come to understand the value of women and their partners receiving Reiki and learning Reiki, preferably early in their pregnancy. What Reiki does is give us an experience of the universal and a connection with our truest self. Harmony, compassion and balance wash over us with Reiki.

And I understand fully the value of a calm pregnancy because I am aware my mother spent a lot of her pregnancy worrying that, like her, I would be born with a physical disability. And that is where I trace back my own need for adrenaline—the familiar environment and territory I grew with in the womb.

Imagine this all around the world. The more children who are born in peace, the more they may seek peace in their lives.

Abimbola Betty Oso

Abimbola Betty Oso is the CEO of Zabeth Isaac design, an exquisite bespoke clothing line that caters to the sophisticated, classy and chic woman. She is a known face within the UK fashion scene with a career spanning more than fifteen years. Abimbola has worked with the award-winning and world renowned designer Adebayo Jones and designed for well-regarded personalities such as OH TV's award winning television presenter Lola Ogunbadejo, founder of Life Changers charity Sheri Adegbesan, and many others. Abimbola also runs Skills for Life, a non-profit organization that helps disadvantaged families in the Northern part of Nigeria that have been affected by the recent bombings. Abimbola is also in the process of launching her website as well as a boutique abroad to cater to her vast amount of international clients. She currently resides in London, is married and blessed with children.

Chapter 12
My Uprising

By Abimbola Betty Oso

Uprising

Relentless in determined inquisition; I wilfully made up my mind to be different. This is the story of the change within me—my uprising.

I was born in the Motherland; West Africa-Nigeria to be precise. The land of milk and honey but no constant electricity. Still, under that duress I grew up in a beautiful environment and had a nice life. I was free, blessed and surrounded by the most loving people in the world-my family.

As a young child I dreamt of walking on a hallway with spectators cheering, clapping hands and in the midst, ladies wearing long beautiful, glittering and glamorously made gowns. As a young child dreaming of this becoming a reality became a regular occurrence; the passion blossomed and the seed was planted in my heart.

I knew what I wanted to do and I was determined to do it. I dreamt about the world understanding and appreciating what I had to offer them. I wanted to be the solution to someone's clothing woes. I respected my vision so much, it comforted me, encouraged me and motivated me. I guess I only really understood the love I had for my craft—it was this that kept me going when confusion, doubt and hurt became the speed bumps which made my journey to success rocky.

Though I am an optimistic person, I was constantly reminded that this world isn't exactly a bed of sweet smelling roses. It can be tough, dark and cold—so as a little girl, I was taught that how you deal with life's shortcomings is what determines if you are ready to chase your dreams or not. I was determined to not just be a dreamer; I wanted more from life, for my future and for myself. What was my dream? Well it was to be an established designer in the world of fashion. Growing up, I loved to stand out with how I dressed. My mother was a seamstress; I never sat under her tutelage though, for my father had a notion that seamstresses were school dropouts. Ironically; he was also the person who advised me to actualise my dreams. I, without any hesitancy, followed his advice and began to sketch dress designs on paper. This was the start of something great; everything began to take shape.

Then an incident occurred that made my desire of becoming a designer in the world of fashion come forth. I witnessed, to my horror, my niece being tortured by the family maid; she tightly covered the little girl in a bathing bowl in an attempt to make it air tight. Her reason for this ludicrous and cruel action; the toddler refused to stop crying. We uncovered the bowl speedily. To the consternation of me and my mother the child was understandably deeply frightened by the horrific experience, she was breathless from the trauma and exhausted from the struggle. We hurriedly took her out of the room. My God, the utter shock and disgust made me shout: furiously, I vowed never to leave my children with a maid (that decision came with a price—I spent most of my days at home being a mother to my wonderful blessings. However it worked in my favour as my kids grew up seeing me (work) sewing at home instilling the notion into their life—"where there's a will there's a way"

I remember years back, the time I was about to get married, a few months before my big day I enrolled as an apprentice at "Faith Fashions". This was my first training in the world of fashion. It was there that I learnt some hand sewing skills and techniques. This was definitely a stepping stone for my progression and growth as a seamstress. My wedding gown was cut whilst undertaking my apprenticeship. I sewed the precious gown together with great excitement. What a delight it was, my dreams were coming true. I must say the finished product was truly a masterpiece and I was so proud of my accomplishment. After my apprenticeship contract expired I enrolled at another sewing class which lasted for eighteen months, I realised that I couldn't actually cut or sew on my own; my trainer usually did all the cuttings overnight and so in the morning all I had to do was sew. Few months after I had my daughter it was challenging; luckily my mother was very supportive,(so my daughter was left under the supervision of my mother once I was off to my new apprenticeship classes). I had to set up a timetable for myself by prioritizing my work on a structured timetable for my classes as well as my home's. As soon as I get home it was time to face my family. This was how I was able to stay focused. Paradoxically, this happened with my three other trainers which I later went on to work with. During my time as an apprentice I also had to run personal errands and do their house-chores. Quite a humbling experience!

Here I am not learning how to sew or cut fabrics even though I have been through six different trainers and I cannot cut or sew a garment on my own. I was introduced to this man after a painstaking research on how thorough he is. He became my seventh trainer—who was trained by a British sartor. During my search for a better trainer, I decided to also enrol for millinery classes then went on to beadwork, knitting pins(was a hobby as a child from the age of six, I went on to learn how to knit with a knitting machine) and finally learned how to tie-dye(it became another passion in my fashion career). This action of continuity increased my knowledge in the world of fashion as it all revolves around fashion (knitting, millinery, beads-which is an accessory) and tie-dye. My advice before I continue, is whatever you're gifted with, make sure you discover and unravel it. The seventh trainer was very different from the others before because he would actually explain himself thoroughly whilst cutting the pattern as well as sewing it, I learnt from him the quote of Ralph Emerson, which suddenly came to mind, "unless you try to do something beyond what you've already mastered, you'll never grow". This sunk in deep and drove me to my expensive venture which paid off. I bought clothes from different boutiques which I loosened in an attempt to see and learn more about how it was put together. My confidence in my craft and knowledge of art of sewing increased significantly. I began to explore within the realm of needlework and experimented; I would use my tie-dye fabrics to recreate what I purchased at the boutiques. Whatever you have as a passion or talent in you should develop it regardless of the obstacles you could come across for it is to make you discover and become a master in. Perseverance is to be your manager, Patience as an assistance while Positivity, your CEO. When we relocated to the United Kingdom I quickly enrolled at Greenwich College to study fashion and clothing. But now my hunger was deeper. I struggled but I discovered that the knowledge I needed alongside college tutorials were buried in books. So I invested in books and more books. This was my breaking point. My breakthrough into the fashion clothing and pattern cutting world, it took me almost 20 years. Also during my challenging years I said to myself "only I can make the good or bad decisions for my life so I choose it to be what I am today" so weigh your actions for by it you'll be judged. That watchword has always been in my heart, mind and head. I kept on setting goals and targets for me to achieve. The change within me occurred when I realized that I can do it—the dream was kept alive and is still living.

Zoë A. Onah

Writer, columnist, coach and public speaker, Zoë A. Onah is the author of the bestseller *Defying the Odds*—one man's struggle and victory over mental illness and his wife whose trust in God never failed. Zoë met her husband, Eze, fourteen years into his tumultuous journey with mental illness. Four years later, he defied the odds with a clean medical bill of no mental illness. Today, they share their experiences and are the voice of hope for mental health and illness. Zoë also co-authored another bestseller with Eze, *Confessions and Meditations for People Facing Mental Health Challenges*.

www.defyingmentalillness.com
www.yookos.com/people/DefyingOddsBook
defyingtheodds@live.co.uk
Defying The Odds Group
@defyingoddsbook

Chapter 13
Why Not Me?

By Zoë A. Onah

E verything of value comes with its own challenges. Wishing away those challenges denies you the opportunity for outstanding rewards. I will start my story from this point. It had been my desire to get married. But when my twenties ended and no knight in shining armour was sweeping me off my feet, I decided I was not going to take neigh for an answer to marriage! By then, my mother, a lady of great tenacity, faith and determination, decided to make her requests for her daughter known before her God whilst I was making my requests known at the wrong places.

Thank God her prayers concerning my "unrighteous causes" were answered, and I soon joined her in making my change in marital status petitions upwards to our heavenly Father. By the time, God decided to hand over my husband to me; I had the maturity to look beyond the wrapping in which he has presented to me! For starters, the brother could not even be asked to clean his car on our first date! Eze, as the brother was called, means king. Could you imagine a king was picking up his potential queen in a chariot that did not say much about the effort or excitement he had put towards this glorious date in history? Well, I decided to overlook this unimpressive oversight and instead focus on the soft eyes of my blind date.

Eze was quick to tell me of his "skeletons" by the second date. Later that night, I was still trying to swallow these bones that had become wedged at the back of my throat. The plan was to call my mother to inform her that it was back to heavenly petitions time. Eze was not the right knight. However, I was grateful for his honesty, which is so vital in relationships, whatever the risks.

Mental health, mental illness, and psychiatry are not always the most palatable words over a cappuccino even in a trendy London coffee bar. Statistics show that 1 in 4 people suffer from mental illness in the UK alone. The figure is real, alive and dwells among us in society. And my date was telling me he was one of those statistics.

Eze was an intelligent achiever with the world at his fingertips when fate decided to dash a cruel hand. Having achieved accolades of prizes and sterling academic achievements, he was suddenly faced with a sentence—life with schizophrenia. As the medical journals will tell you, there is no cure. He was faced with uncertain prospects of a life of medication, hospitals and a far below substandard life. During his first episode he ended up in a psychiatric hospital and was signed off work for a year. His life that had been sporting along was now suddenly on reverse gears.

Mum did not buy into my back to prayer petitions, so I continued my courtship with Eze. After a whirlwind romance, I got the diamond on my left finger and was faced with the stark reality of what I had signed up for! Not many days after the engagement, my raw eyes witnessed very clearly a magnified reality of mental illness. Cruel, relentless and unpredictable; Eze was ill; he seemed shut up in a silent incomprehensible world.

Mental illness is not often tattooed on the foreheads of sufferers; in fact, it never is. Unusual behaviour can make sufferers identifiable, but is not always the obvious rule of thumb. The latter was the case for Eze. It is a disease that does not distinguish by class, gender, status, education or race. It can be a silent enemy among us. One that tears families apart; that causes heartache, that takes the last squeezed drop of energy lynched out of carers, that divides family loyalty, that leaves children asking unanswered questions, that makes employers seem like dragons, that has society scorn sufferers like vipers.

How could this happen to Eze? To my dream wedding? To our future? Well, it did. And why me after all that heavenly bombardment? God does not necessarily give us what we think we deserve, but what is in His plan for us.

Eze's story was to last 18 long, winding years. I met Eze in the fourteenth year of that journey; a journey of dark valleys and steep mountains. But even the longest road has turns. Eze's journey would finally end through our faith in God, a strong network of supporters, and my love for my husband and my trust in God.

Life will throw you a few curved balls, you must be prepared to catch them and be the winner.

There are many messages in my short story today. One is on marriage. If you are single, throw away the long list of who you think Mr. Right should be and have an open and willing heart. Like me, your king may not come in the package you desire. True kings come in disguises, so don't be fooled by Mr. Porsche Muscle Fine Man. Marriage also has a purpose. It goes beyond the candle lit dinners and country drives we dream of. One purpose of my marriage is being fulfilled today as advocates for the voice of mental health in giving people a hope.

Hold on to your faith. Your faith will be tested. Challenges build character. The difference between charcoal and diamond is pressure. They are both made of the same substance. Which would you rather be? Would you shirk at the size of the so called Goliath that stood before you, or would you run towards the giant with a sling in your hand, knowing that this big Goliath only makes it easier for you not to miss your target? I wanted to get the king's reward, but it meant not being intimidated by giants.

The next thing is that a delay is not a denial. I know it sounds like a cliché we all have heard, and I was even cringing as I wrote it! David killed Goliath but the young lad had to wait several years before he became king.

Each birthday looked like my wish was becoming more of a denial. But those years were training years. I was by no means ready to face the challenges of this walk in overcoming mental illness. God knew what lay ahead and prepared me. When the going got tough, if it had been back in the wrong days, I would have balked with a trail of dust behind me. I don't deny those thoughts came, but I was by then made of diamond material. Don't pray away that challenge. Mandela stuck to his convictions, he endured suffering and today, his name is in the annals of history.

If you pray for God to take away the challenge, He may just do as He did with Elijah. All God did was replace the prophet with a successor. God's will cannot be terminated. Let the purpose that has been placed in you stay no matter what. Refuse the easy way out.

As I said earlier, wrappings are immaterial. This not only applies to single ladies but to everything in life. Let us look beyond the packaging of things. It is what's in the package that counts. Anyone can put expensive wrapping paper over something cheap.

Remember that you are a powerhouse. It took just four years of being a helpmate to my husband for him to overcome through faith in God, the challenge of fourteen prior years of mental illness. Don't underestimate the power inside you to make things happen, especially as a lady. A great woman of God once said, "Men are the head, but women are the neck." That means our influence is powerful.

Tenacity means having unlimited visions. Have a picture of what you want to see. For Eze and me, we kept looking, reading and listening to the Word of God. You are what you read, see and listen to. The Internet and the statistics were putting fear in my heart. Why swallow fear when you can digest faith?

And finally, mental illness is real. It does not discriminate, and we all have a part to play in fighting the stigma and discrimination that comes with this disease to make it more bearable for those suffering. If you are challenged with it, know that there is no end to the soul of man. That means you can achieve and be anything you want to be. Let this be your mindset. I had the support of a beautiful church and my family, which made a BIG difference. Tenacity requires people cheering you on, encouraging you to get to the finish line.

Today, I can look back and say THANK GOD. I would not be writing to you right now otherwise. The furnace of our trials extracted the true elements in us and brought Eze and I out shining. My husband and I can say WHY NOT US instead of WHY US? For God indeed turned our broken pieces into masterpieces. Tenacity will see you through. And DEFY THE ODDS!

Why NOT you?

Antonetta Fernandes

Antonetta Fernandes is a highly sought after self-esteem life coach/ mentor and motivational speaker. She has also contributed to successful regeneration partnerships with communities and businesses both nationally and internationally. Dynamic skills and passion have driven her global philanthropic projects in Goa, Brazil, West Africa, Uganda and Mauritius. She is a great believer that charity begins at home, so she completed the Dublin Marathon raising £3000 for Whizz Kids. She graduated from the Academy of Wealth and Achievement as a Master Results Coach/NLP Master Practitioner and Hypnotherapist. Antonetta's mission is to elevate and transform women to realize and live with passion.

www.antonettafernandes.co.uk
antonetta@antonettafernandes.co.uk
tinyurl.com/kz5qst2
@Fabasia
uk.linkedin.com/pub/dir/Antonetta/Fernandes

Chapter 14
Every Mountain Matters, Embrace the Difference

By Antonetta Fernandes

I was 15 when I arrived at one of the orphanage homes, away from family and friends, feeling so alone, frightened and lost, with tears uncontrollably pouring down my face—and it hit me. I was being punished for running away from mental and physical abuse from a family friend.

This person came into our lives at a time when my parents were struggling to bring up nine children on a very low income. Sometimes all they could feed us was bread and tea or milk. He helped us financially and also helped to enrol my siblings into school for reduced fees. It was at this time I felt I had to get a job to support the family. Other girls my age in the community were earning money from working in the city, or so I thought. However, as hard as I tried, the jobs were not coming my way. But this was my solace; being out searching kept me away from home, away from my abuser.

His advances became unbearable, as he would either beat me with a stick or feel me up. Finally, I lied saying I had a job so that I could stay out longer and not return home until he had left; but I could not sustain this, because at the end of the month I did not have a salary. The final straw was to stay with friends. My parents were heartbroken, and at the time I really did not understand just how much. After a few years, my youngest brother committed suicide, followed by my father a year later, and finally brother Peter who died 13 years ago of lung cancer. What I saw in my mother's eyes is an image I will carry forever.

"You need to keep on going, no matter what the mountain in front of you is. You didn't't dwell on the WHY, but cherished the rope that held you up." I recall this saying from my grandmother. Edelvale was the first mountain I climbed. It was difficult at first, the culture shock, loneliness, taunts and worthlessness began to kick in, but my determination to climb out of this hellhole won the nuns over. So much so that they funded my fees to attend one of the top Catholic schools, where I completed my studies. My time in Edevale brought me many blessings, and brought out many of my hidden talents. The artist in me surfaced, and one of my first claims to fame was when I won an art competition and appeared in the local newspaper. My determination and a "not-dwelling-on-the-past" attitude led to this achievement.

In 1974 at 21, I got married and later that year, immigrated to England. One of the happiest moments in my life was the day my son was born. I felt wholesome, magical and rejoiced at the great miracle I had received. My life was changing, my family was complete and finally I had it all. Both my husband and I worked very hard; we were not rich but fairly comfortable. We immersed ourselves in family and work, and organized charitable social events with like-minded individuals to fund projects around the world. One of the important campaigns I took on as editor for a community newsletter was against Child Sex Trade in Goa, India. We created global awareness of this, collecting 9338 signatures in the UK. At the same time, my career blossomed as my quest for learning, combined with my skills and ever increasing knowledge, and enabled me to flourish. I felt I had arrived at "Destination Success"—at least that is what I thought.

A few days after celebrating our 25th wedding anniversary the bubble burst and the fairy tale ended. My husband and son were the objects of this hurt, but I had to acknowledge that I had no doubt been a contributor. On the day before my hysterectomy surgery, I received a letter from an acquaintance whom I had known as a child and who went to social gatherings I used to attend that things has been happening behind my back and she wanted me to before someone else tell me. It was a very challenging time of my life.

Waking up in a hospital ward in the still of the night, I reflected on some truths that I had avoided coming to terms with. Was this all a dream? Was it a nightmare from which I would awaken and everything would be fine? The night nurse came to check on me and sensing there was something wrong, asked if the pain was bearable. My pain was of a broken heart and no amount of morphine would be enough to wipe it out.

After my surgery I was discharged to the care of my husband and son with strict instruction from the medics that I was to rest for the next three months without even lifting a kettle. I was forced to take time out; my body was speaking to me, and I knew that I could not bury my head in the sand but must climb the toughest and highest mountain of all. Like manna from heaven I received a bouquet of white lilies and several books from my boss, including *The 7 Habits of Highly Effective People* by Stephen Covey and Susan Jefferson's *Feel the Fear and Do It Anyway*. I applied these principles to heal my wounds and move forward.

My marriage ended in 2000, but we both supported our son by getting him therapy and implants to help wean him off the drugs. There was no expense spared; even with mounting credit card debt we soldiered on. It would work for a few months and he would relapse. This was not easy for his father to face and we did not understand drug addiction. So I took on this role of looking after my son and decided to try a deep home detox to support his recovery. The will to want to come off drugs is an individual choice, and willpower and determination go hand-in-hand.

On a crisp day in February 2005 we were blessed with a granddaughter. My determination grew even stronger then to find a way to support my son and his partner. I was searching for a solution, which came to me as I was passing the Ibis Hotel in Fulham. I walked towards the reception curious to know why so many people were gathered there. Even though I had not registered for this jam-packed event I managed to find a kind soul to give me a ticket.

This 3-day event had a profound effect on my future thinking. I applied what I had learned there, about the power of manifestation using detailed visualization. As if like magic I won £7000 of training through the Academy of Wealth & Achievement. I qualified as an NLP Master Practitioner, Hypnotherapist, Life Coach and a platform speaker. The journey with my son took me to a path of infinite possibilities and now at the age of 62, I am enjoying the universal benefits bestowed upon me of love, joy, peace and happiness.

As a child I dreamt of a kingdom of magic, with fairies, rainbows, spaceships, and unicorns. It was a place of peace where love overflowed, joy mirrored every reflection, happiness glowed and purity just rained. Since then I have searched the Internet in a quest to discover tools for my magical kingdom.

I travelled and learned from transformational masters, healers and gurus to create this universal magical kingdom to empower others. These tools have helped me to build my business, where self-esteem and confidence operate from a place of high pulsating energy, love and joy. Self-esteem is the key ingredient in my products and services for women, the fundamental power that juices all areas of our lives. Be it wealth, health, spirituality, joy, career or relationships, my mission is to elevate and transform women to realize and live their passion. So hop on the train to Self-Esteem City. Enter a fun packed playground with a galaxy of transformational tools. Every tool in the universal playground is hallmarked and oozing with wonderful self-creation.

Bukola Orija

Buky Buky Orija is a business and life coach and the Director of Dominion Business Solution Ltd. She is also an ambassador of La Proverbs Ltd, a coaching, mentoring and personal development company. She loves working with people to achieve both their personal and corporate goals. Prior to this, she worked in various departments in the banking sector with an emphasis on customer satisfaction. Her wealth of experience in banking has equipped her with invaluable transferable skills.

Olubukola Ellen Orija, a.k.a Buky, is a wife and mother of three grown children.

bukyorija@yahoo.com
facebook.com/bukola.orija

Chapter 15
My Story

By Bukola Orija

M y name is Olubukola Ellen Orija, I was born in ile-ife, in osun
state, had most of my childhood in the area, went to college and
university in Oyo and Lagos state, all in western part of Nigeria.

My late father was a polygamist, I am the fourth child of the ten
children, my mother had five children, I am the third child and third
girl from my mother and have a brother and a younger sister.

My childhood

My parent were illiterate, I grew up in a family where love does not
exist, poverty was written everywhere, it was a struggle to eat, clothes
and shoes were luxury and all I could remember was seeing my mother
constantly struggling for us to have food on the table and was subjected
to all sort of abuse, mentally, physically, emotionally, financially, etc.
She is so gentle, soft spoken, woman of faith that strongly belief in
marriage tie and God. As I see her living her life in such condition, I
said to myself that when I grow up, I will make sure my mother have a
quality life for the rest of her life and she is living it now.

My father was too busy with his other business to notice his family. As
a child I get more beating from than love, my two senior sisters were
given away to live with different relatives in the state capital, that is
Lagos, Nigeria at a tender age. Living with relations seriously affected
their personal development. I was privilege to visit them during holiday

with my daddy; I and realised they were living in a lovely home and have nice and regular meals, but I hated how they were being treated. They were left to do all domestic chores at home with no time to go to school. I value my education so much and I said to myself that I will never live with any family member but remain with my mother until I completed my education and I will support my senior sisters to come back to my mother and complete their education.

When I completed my primary education, I was left on my own to process my admission to high school but not until a year after, there was no support from my parent and no one to guide me through. I got admitted the following year to a girls boarding school, Ife Girls' High School, life was tougher very difficult in the hostel, meals were not better, there were daily punishment from all seniors, bullying was acceptable, it was very tough for me in my junior years but I have to endure to complete my education.

As I was growing up, my father never lived with us; he was in Lagos city with his second wife and only visited occasionally. During one of his visit after my high school he decided to take me to a friend who was a principal of teacher training college without discussing with me. He decided with his friend for me to live with him (his friend) and to be trained as a teacher. Since I hated to live with any other person, seeing my sister's ordeal, I declined immediately and he was very mad at me and mentioned he will forsake me as his child if I choose to have my way. To me that was a better option, I agreed with him to forsake me as his child and he took me back to my mother. Because of my choice, we were abandoned; he neither visited nor sends money for almost one year.

Life was tough; my mother had to engage in all sort of buying and selling businesses from fruits to daily product for us to survive. She practically sold most of her clothes and personal belonging to raise money for me and my siblings to survive, she make sure we never go hungry, we always have food on the table.

I knew I wanted a higher education but not to be a teacher. I have to mature and develop quickly to stand for what I believe and have to make several enquiries and process my admission to college on my own.

I finally got admitted to The Polytechnic, Ibadan in Oyo state even though I did not know the course to study then.

During the admission process, I mention to the course advisor to choose any course that my results qualify for and he mentioned to me that I qualify to study Banking and Finance. I had no idea of what it meant but got fascinated as he explained to me the opportunity of getting the professional banking examination after my college and life as a qualified banker that means working in a corporate environment in high street with prestige and financial stability. I said to myself, yes, that is what I want.

I needed to pay my tuition fees and my mother could not afford it, I went up to my father, as a forsaken child to beg and informed him about my the admission, he was excited and paid for everything and since them he was responsible for my education, never question my bill and started bounding with him.

Now that my father financing my education, I had enough money and I contacted my second sister if interested to continue with her education somewhere else, she agreed with me and I arranged a new boarding school for her and relocated her, took up the responsible for her education from whatever I got from my father, she was three years older than me but five years behind in her education, I supported to change her story.

I registered immediately with the professional body, Chartered Institute of Bankers. I choose to study for both college and the professional examination at the same time. It was a hard choice, but I gave myself a goal of five years of hard work to become a graduate and a chartered banker.

Challenges ahead of me were:

1. To commune every other day between two cities to attend
2. As a full time student in college, I needed 95% attendance to graduate.
3. I needed accommodation in Lagos when I come for my professional examination and the only opportunity was to stay with family member.

4. I needed finances for my transport and study materials.

Survivor strategies

1. I got a friend that wanted the materials for professional lectures but unable to attend lectures in the city as there was no one to accommodate him, he choose to support my transport fare while I get all the study materials for him.
2. I choose to stay with an uncle and made him understand that I needed time for my classes and also sleep over in some of my friend's house and most times go to our pastor's house for meal.
3. I have to travel with all sort of vans transporting newspapers to other cites at early hours, about 4.00 am, because it was the cheapest
4. I had financial and materials support from fellow students in the professional class as they were all working full time in banks.

I witnessed progressive success each year as I studied for both examinations. I remained focus to my goals and looking forward to graduate and get my banking professional qualification, at the end of the fifth year, June 1987, I graduated from my college and sat for the last paper in my professional examination in September same year. I passed my final paper and qualified as Chartered Banker, ACIB, in September 1987, that was 'a Dream come true'.

I started my first job at First Bank of Nigeria plc, as a national youth service corps member, I got a full time job within one month of completing the national program at Wema Bank Plc, Lagos and subsequently worked with 3 other banks for 18years.

I knew I did not have a life as a child, but my upbringing has actually helped me to cope with the challenges in my life, my marriage and career.

I grew up:

- With a strong character
- To know exactly what I want and go for it.
- To develop faster than my age, have to take adult decision for myself and to change my sister's story

- Staying power
- Willing power
- Had to change my mother's story and give her quality life
- Not to allow any circumstances to affect me negatively.

I was able to cope with my busy career as a professional banker, a mother of three, a leader in church and a wife.

I stayed focused, had the strength to cope and maintain my position in my marriage and see my children becoming a responsible adult despite all challenges.

I know I am not there yet, I look for every opportunity for my personal development.

My goal is to support women that are hurt in marriage.

Word of encouragement

I want to encourage anyone in a similar situation that if I can survive all odds to get to the top of my career, you too can!!!

Always have a written goal and dream big, you can achieve whatever your mind conceives. You will get there.

YOU CAN!!!

Usha Oliver

Usha Oliver is a widely sought-after international speaker, confidence coach, and training and development consultant, who is passionate about uncovering potential, especially that which is latent.

She speaks at a variety of events, as she focuses on finding ways to help people and organisations maximise their potential. Her books *"I Dared To Dream"* and *"Citadel of Hope"* are scheduled to be released in the summer of 2014.

For more information on Usha Oliver, please visit www.dtod.co.uk

Chapter 16
From Overwhelmed To Overcomer

S ome of you reading this might be thinking, "Oh, it's alright for you. I can't do what you've done. I'm not a strong woman. I can't forgive. Do you have any idea, how much they hurt me? I need to make sure that nobody else can do that to me!"

Anyone who makes light of forgiveness, and says it is easy—is either being dishonest, or has never had to forgive anyone. The latter is very unlikely. It might be helpful to bear in mind, what forgiveness isn't. It is necessary get rid of false substitutes, and wrong ideas of forgiveness. I have found out that:

Forgiveness is not forgetting—that is amnesia.

I read of Lisa Goertz, who lost her family in the Jewish holocaust. Before she escaped Germany, she saw a vision of Jesus, and became a Christian. In her vision, she saw Jesus—a fellow Jew—suffering on the cross or the sins of humanity. In her book *"I Stepped Into Freedom"*, she recalls her losses (of her husband, son, daughter and mother), and says,

"But there is no bitterness or hatred in my heart; one cannot live with bitterness and hatred. There is the peace of God in me, and a reflection of His divine love which makes me love my fellow-men whether they are black or yellow or white, whether they are Jews or Christians, whether they belong to this denomination or that."

Forgiveness is not avoidance, or making light of things we find hurtful.

Being imperfect people, there are many things that constantly happen between us and others, that can be either major issues, or minor irritations. We can ignore the minor. But when the hurt is real, it does not help to claim "It doesn't matter". It does not help to dismiss something that is wrong.

Dwight Small in *Design for Christian Marriage* says,

"Forgiveness is not merely a soft attitude toward a harsh fact."

Forgiveness is not excusing.

Forgiveness does not deny that the one who has caused the hurt, is responsible for their actions. We can make allowances for people's behaviour. But there is a tendency to err too much in that direction. To do so, amounts to lessening our dignity as human beings. We are created in the image of God, who calls us to account for our moral choices. If we are to grow, we must accept responsibility for our own part in that process.

C. S. Lewis, says in *Fernseeds and Elephants*:

"If one was really not to blame, then there is nothing to forgive. In that sense, forgiveness and excusing are almost opposite."

We have seen some examples of what forgiveness isn't. So, what *is* forgiveness? This is what I have learned.

Forgiveness means that we do not let the past dominate the future.

Forgiveness means to "let go". This has nothing with putting something out of your mind. There may be some memories that we are unable to put out of our minds, but we can choose not to allow them control our attitudes—even towards those who may be responsible for those memories. It means we don't let past experiences dominate our future, and/or prevent us from becoming all that God has planned for us.

Forgiveness means to "cancel a debt".

Forgiveness is freedom.

It is the miracle of a new beginning.

It is to start where we are, not where we wish we were, or the other person was.

It is to hold out a hand; to want to renew a friendship; to want a new relationship with husband, father, daughter, friend, or even enemy.

It may not take away the hurt. It will not re-write the past, or deny the injury. It does not ignore the possibility and need for repentance, and a change in the relationship.

Forgiveness means being willing to take the initiative in dealing with any barriers to a restored relationship. It means that I am willing to have a relationship with the other party based on Christian love, and not on what happened in the past if the response of the other person makes it possible.

"Forgiveness is the vital act of love, seeking to restore the harmony that has been shattered"—Dwight Small (Design for Christian Marriage).

Joyce Meyer tells of how she was repeatedly sexually abused by her father, as a child. After she made Jesus the Lord of her life, she forgave her father. She paid for his nursing care, till the end of his life.

It is also important to know that although forgiveness *may* lead to reconciliation, they are not the same.

A great freelance writer, tells of the devastation she suffered, when her father left her mother to marry his secretary. She was 12 years old. Years later, she asked Jesus Christ to be the Lord of her life. She forgave her father. She began to write him letters. Sometimes, he responded with hateful letters—but she chose to forgive him, each time. He died 25 years later. Just before he died, he said, "I'm glad you forgave me."

We may say, "Well, doesn't this prove that forgiveness means ignoring the past? What about justice?"

Forgive anyone who does you wrong, just as Christ has forgiven you—
Colossians 3:13

God is perfect in both love, and justice. God invented forgiveness in order to keep His romance with fallen humanity, alive. His justice was fully satisfied at Calvary. Forgiveness always comes at a cost. When we forgive someone who has hurt us, in a sense, we accept responsibility for the consequence of their sin against us.

The Hebrew word for 'forgive' means two things: to remit a debt, and to pay it.

However hard we may try to live peaceably with others (Romans 12:18), not all attempts at reconciliation, are successful.

Yes, they may have hurt you badly. Maybe, they took advantage of you when you were a child. And you resent them for it. Yet, harbouring resentment has been linked to a number of physical and mental complaints. I have heard someone say that "resentment is like drinking poison, and waiting for your enemy to die". Forgiveness has to happen, if you must arrive at healing.

The story is told of Gracilla Martinez who learned to forgive when her 15 year-old son, was executed. The boy had recently become a Christian, and he told her, "Don't hate them. Forgive them, Mamacita. Forgive them, or they will be the victors." But she could not. She carried her hatred in her heart, actively plotting retaliation, for 10 years. She says she finally forgave when she saw how destructive her hatred was—it consumed her energy, crippled her friendships, and disabled any good she tried to do. She says, "I finally saw the truth of my son's last words, that when we return hatred to those who hate us, we fall into playing their game according to their rules—and do them the great favour of hurting ourselves."

Dear friends, don't try to get even. Let God take revenge—Romans 12: 19

You cannot be an overcomer, if you have excess baggage. Unforgiveness *is* excess baggage.

The thing about walls is that they keep people out, or in. The wall you've built to keep others out, has locked you in. The Lord wants to be your Protector, but He can't do that, if you're too busy trying to protect yourself. God didn't promise that you would never get hurt. But He will heal you, if you come to Him—rather than try to take care of everything, yourself. If you have built walls around you, you must tear them down in faith. Go to Jesus wiith each old wound, and receive His healing. When someone hurts you, don't let it fester. Take it to God, and be willing to handle it His way—instead of your way.

There is a particular Scripture that I have found really helpful, in learning to let go—Jeremiah 30:17

> *For I will restore health to you, and I will heal your wounds, says the Lord, because they have called you an outcast, saying, This is* [fill in your name] *whom no one seeks after and for whom no one cares.*

If you forgive, you won't just *survive* the hurt. You will become stronger, *thrive*, and be able to minister to others.

So, tear down those walls, today!

Copright © Usha Oliver, 2014
Usha's book, CITADEL OF HOPE is due to be released in the summer of 2014

Sandra Nelson

Sandra Nelson is a qualified linguist, well-established financial advisor, and the founder & CEO of Lift Effects. She is a highly acclaimed Life Lifter specialist.

From a very early age she possessed an innate desire to improve the lives of everyone she came in contact with. She maintains a simple goal of helping individuals become the very best version of themselves, and it was out of this passion that Lift Effects was established. Through Lift Effects, she and her team have created an outlet to communicate strength, energy, positivity, purpose and passion. Over the years Lift Effects has made a tangible difference in the lives of many, and Sandra's name has become synonymous with life lifter, coach and mentor.

Chapter 17
Going Down Memory Lane

By Sandra Nelson

I am not a prisoner of my past, nor do I regret the things that I have done or the failures of yesteryears. Quite the contrary, in fact, these memories serve as a reminder of how far I have come and spur me to go even further.

December 6, 2012 is a date that will forever remain etched in my mind, as it marked the birth of a new purpose within my life. On that particular day I picked up a copy of the Metro Newspaper, and was drawn to an article on the forty-fifth page, which was headlined the "happiest woman is killed by loneliness." The story explained how a confident, glamorous and seemingly happy young lady, who was constantly surrounded by friends and family, was in reality, depressed, lonely and tragically suicidal. As the article continued, it elaborated on the woman's excellent educational achievements and her promising future, which sadly never happened.

As I looked at the picture of this beautiful young lady, the emptiness in her eyes struck me and I knew instantly that her death had been caused by a loss of purpose and lack of understanding of the true meaning of life. Right then and there I said to me, "if this lady had come into contact with someone like me, this tragedy would never have occurred." All my life I've possessed an intrinsic desire to leave people better than how they were when I met them. This desire is fuelled by my ability to recognise the greatness in people, even within the unlikeliest of individuals.

As I continued reading the article, it began stirring up memories inside me. Surprising though it may seem, once upon a time I had been just like this lady. There had been many occasions in my past when in the midst of my many friends and family, I would feel an emptiness, a void deep within. At the time I did not realize that this void could not be filled by anyone or anything. It was not until much later in life that I came to know that the gaping hole could only be filled by discovering who I really was; but once I had unearthed this truth, my life changed for the better.

As I continued my stroll down memory lane, I recalled a conversation a friend and I had when we were in secondary school. We were no more than 11 years old at the time, but I distinctly remember her telling me that I was so dark, that no man would ever want to marry me, as men did not like dark skinned ladies. As she spoke those words, something rose up within me and I challenged her, asking who exactly had told her this. I defiantly continued by informing my friend that I was, in fact, a very beautiful girl who every man would love to marry. This is something I recited to myself in front of the mirror over the years, and is something that actually became a reality as I grew older. In the year 2000 I won my school beauty pageant, and also went on to be part of the top 10 national Lux beauty pageant finalists.

This scenario from my past highlights exactly how life is shaped by what you say and believe. At the time my friend and I had this conversation, I had not yet known the true power of words. But even from that early age, I rightly challenged her misconceptions about beauty, and the end result was my life becoming synonymous with my words.

It is so important to say what you want to see in your life. I used to tell myself that I would not have to look long for a job, I would have the best marriage, I would host the biggest ladies' conferences, and I would also change lives—so much so that people would want to identify with me; and this has always been the case. I may not be the most beautiful lady on the surface of the earth, but I have become a beautiful lady both inside and out.

In 1990 when I was just 15 years old, I was involved in a very serious car accident in which a close friend of mine lost her life. Those we were travelling with also suffered multiple injuries, but I managed to vacate the car unscathed. At the time of the incident we were on our way to a party in a different city, so I had not told my parents. The first time they knew about my location was when they received a phone call informing them that I had been involved in a fatal accident. The news of this accident spread across town like wildfire, and I became too ashamed to be associated with anyone. I felt like a social pariah, as anytime I was with my friends and their parents came around, they would give me a judgmental look that disapproved of their children being associated with a "naughty, party girl" like me. The irony of the situation was that this party would have been my first, but we never made it there.

It was equally hard going back to school, as the accident was the hot topic there too. The main thing that pushed me back into school was my genuine love of education. As I went back to school I began to receive many invitations to parties from friends as well as strangers who had heard about me. I suddenly became the girl that everyone wanted to party with. I eventually decided to accept these invitations, after all, I had already been labelled as the "party girl", so I thought I might as well live up to this name. In hindsight I can see how I failed to recognise the gift of life that had been bestowed upon me when I survived the accident. I did not appreciate what I had and so did nothing with it.

My story could have gone on like this, identical to the life of the young lady I read about in the Metro, with parties, friends and happiness on the outside, but with loneliness slowly killing me on the inside; but this is why Lift Effects was founded—to help people find their passion and purpose in improving themselves as well as the lives of others. Without helping people, I believe there is no purpose, no passion, no destiny to fulfil, only isolation and bareness.

I recall another fateful night after a party, when a guy approached my friend and offered her a ride home; she accepted and I went with her. Halfway through the journey the car pulled over and the guys ordered us to exit the vehicle in the middle of nowhere. Their demeanour had completely changed. At point I was not sure what would become of us, but suddenly a group of men came marching along the road out of nowhere holding machetes and singing a song.

They were pushing us all, raising their machetes and singing. So many thoughts ran through my mind mainly that this is how it would all end. If only I had not attended the party, I would not have been subjected to this ordeal. Thankfully though, one of the men in the group understood English, and we explained that we were supposed to be in school. So we had to act like we were friends with the boys, but the men decided to take us to the police station where we were made to wait until the morning before they let us go. For a second time, I was granted the gift of life and yet again failed to do anything with it.

At some stage I began to realize all the partying was not giving me any fulfilment or satisfaction, but I was unable to tell anyone I was not having fun, and so I carried on. Right in the midst of friends, I lost the enthusiasm to live and the will to carry on. I put on the facade of someone who was very happy with high self-esteem, but I was actually very low. It was at this point I realized that having friends, a boyfriend, and engaging in social activities did not automatically fill the voids in my life.

After a while I made the decision that enough was enough, and I started rehearsing how to tell my friends that I would no longer be travelling from city to city in search of fun with them. The pressure of what to say and how I would say it was immense, as was the anticipation of how my decision was to be received by my friends. When I eventually built up the courage to tell them, they did not take it lightly. One of my closest friends at the time tried her best to persuade me to change my mind, but I stood my ground.

I made the decision to move to the UK in 2003. I remember catching up with some of my university friends, and informing them of my career plans and other things that I wanted to achieve in life. I was taken aback by the response of one friend in particular, who told me it would be impossible to get a job in the banking industry. When I queried the logic behind his statement, his response was to simply touch his skin, referring to the supposed disadvantage of my skin colour.

The more I spent time with this crowd, the more their thoughts and views influenced me. Another friend of mine (who later became my husband), noticed this change in me and encouraged me to follow my vision. Consequently I decided to trade my old friends in for new friends who believed anything was possible regardless of skin colour; as a result, my speech and mentality changed. From that point onwards I maintained the anything is possible attitude, and within three months I got a job at a bank. My friends were amazed and could not believe I got the dream job. From there it was from one promotion after another.

From that experience I learned that the friends that you keep are so important. Oftentimes we place too much emphasis on how long we have been friends with someone, rather than the quality of the friendship. As I began my new life in the UK I had to make a decision about the people I spent my time with, regardless of whether we were childhood friends or not. Sometimes you have to sacrifice some friends in order to fulfil your purpose and destiny. I had to make a similar decision when I became a born again Christian. I had to put a stop to the time I spent with friends who were unable to comprehend my new found faith. There was little respect for what I believed in from some of my friends at the time. They were hoping that my beliefs would be a passing phase and that I would return to my old ways. The decisions you make today will most certainly determine your future.

In a nutshell, these experiences helped to shape my life, and made me realize that the decisions we take in life can either build us up or destroy us. I learned that life is a most precious gift, and when we are given something meaningful, we are obligated to do something with it.

Emptiness and loneliness do not disappear because of marriage, friends, or material things; they will only go away once you have found your purpose, which will lead you to your destiny. Your purpose must be connected to helping people, identifying needs and meeting those needs; without helping people there is no purpose.

Life is a journey. For some it takes longer and for others it's shorter. Regardless of what happens on your journey or what you stop to do, you just have to stay on the path until you get to your destination.

Anne Arouna

Anne Arouna was born in Africa in a polygamous Muslim family among several siblings.

Anne encountered all kinds of abuses from trusted families and friends, and suffered greatly as a result. Thinking that getting married would ease her pain, she got married to the first man that came along, a polygamous man.

Unfortunately, things worsened as she wrongly accused, rejected, beaten, battered and starred. She went through so much pain, anguish and hurts for many years, and even suffered depression at one point. At the end of it all, her husband left her with her young son to fend for themselves.

One night, Anne had a spiritual encounter that marked her journey in her new found faith of Christianity that led her to forgive wholeheartedly all those who had hurt and harmed her throughout her life.

Anne is at peace with every one of her abusers that are still alive today. Anne uses her experience to teach and empower others in particular abusers ladies, that there is so much power, freedom and joy in forgiveness even to those who have abused you.

Anne is a Teacher by profession Holding a degree in French Studies and also a PGCE. She speaks over 10 different languages. She enjoys cooking and writing. Anne is working for the Lord in her church Ministry.

Awaroubatou@ yahoo.com
Awaroubatou@hotmail.com

Chapter 18
Anne Arouna's Story

By Anne Arouna

I grew up in a strict Muslim family in Africa. My father had many wives, and my mother was the first wife. Her role was to stay in the village while her husband lived with the youngest spouse in the city. I had many brothers and sisters but I was the eldest girl in the family.

Growing up, I did not have a happy childhood because I was separated from my mum at the age of five and taken to the city to live with my dad. When I was fifteen years old, something terrible happened to me. I was sexually abuse and I could not tell anyone, and I know nobody would have believed me.

Later, my father died and I went back to the village to stay with my mother. I was happy to be with my mum but another incident took place whilst I was in the village

A few years later, I met a handsome man and fell in love. He was older than me, but I had a crush on him and he was my brother's friend too. That relationship ended in a dramatic way too

Many years passed and I could not trust any man. I did not want anyone near me anymore. My mother told me that I needed to have someone in my life and get married. I travelled to France because my brother invited me to come and pursue my studies. Even leaving my native country to another developed one did not help matters. I was completely lost in my mind and I almost took my own live.

Due to this experience, I was sent back to Africa only three months after my arrival in France. I was devastated and lost. I stopped eating and could not sleep. I lost all hope.

In my despair, decided to get married to a man who already has other wives according to Islamic law. Most people would think my ordeal would have ended by this time but "NO", it was simply another journey on a whole new level. Being a wife and living with others who you have to share your husband with is another mentally, physically and emotionally experience for me.

I ended up finding a job, and one of my colleagues was a Christian. She noticed that I cried in silence, but one day she confronted me and wanted to know why. As a Muslim, I did not like Christians. In fact, I hated them. My colleague knew that, but she still showed me love and care. She insisted that I tell her what was going on. As I told her what my challenges are. After I narrated my story to her, she laughed and said that this matter was so simple for Jesus to handle.

I told her that she should not call Jesus into my problem, but she kept on telling me to try Jesus for only one day and see if he would not show up. She was as bold and confident as she spoke to me. I was shocked to see someone who really believes so much in Jesus and not God. She said that in this problem, Jesus was the only final solution. She encouraged me to tell Jesus about what I wanted. In fact, I wanted reconciliation with my husband.

As soon as I reached home I told him that if he reconciles my husband and me I would promise to follow him all my life. Amazingly, my husband came home that night to reconcile with me. I could not believe my experience of the divine intervention of the Lord. I saw the Lord's mighty hands in my life.

Despite this miracle, I still had a hole in my heart because of my inner wounds. I was so hurt and could not forgive those who destroyed my life. I

I kept my new faith away from everybody, and asked Jesus to keep me as his secret disciple; and He did it. I kept my faith unknown to people until ten years later when my husband discovered my little secret of which lead to our divorce because of my new faith.

I made the right decision. It was all about Jesus and not man. I was abandoned and humiliated again, but the Lord was on my side, guiding me into truth. I was still hurt and kept on carrying the burden of sorrows and a broken heart. Each time I looked at the scar on my heart, I could not stop weeping.

My journey in the Christian faith had begun. I was hungry and thirsty to know Jesus more than ever. Something in me was missing. I went from church to church looking for that truth about my Lord. Jesus was the same yesterday, today and forever. One day I came to a church where the Word of God was preached with revelation. Through the Word, I was able to let go of my pain, hurt and abuse by forgiving the people who put me in those situations. I thought I forgave them but I did not, and I could not move forward because of it. My past kept on haunting me until I truly understood that I had to let go.

In the end, knowing Jesus has taught me how to move on in life through forgiveness. Bitterness was not the solution, nor revenge. This hurt and lack of forgiveness went on for a long time in my life. They affected everything about me. I had no confidence and lost all my self-esteem. This took me about 40 years, but Jesus took only one day to transform my life. I was shown that surrendering everything to my Saviour was the only option.

I thank God that all things worked for my good. I was chosen to tell my story in order to help other women who did not know how to get out of similar situations. It happens by forgiving and letting go. But someone has to show how to be healed.

Today, I am touching lives with my testimony. I am not ashamed to tell the world my story and about how the Lord chose me from Islam to become a Christian. I am doing mighty things for the Lord.

This is the reason why I developed a passion for writing, because I need to tell my story to help other women. Our stories will always be unique because we are all different. We are indeed privileged to be called "Daughter of Zion" because there is something particular about us. We are saved to save others.

Maureen Pearson (Maureen P)

Maureen Pearson (Maureen P) is a sort-after a recording artist with great success in the music industry. She came from a music-loving family and this has aided her journey in the industry. By taking things easy, Maureen performs at high profile events all around the UK. Some of her work can be found on Youtube.

Chapter 19
My Journey

Maureen Pearson

My journey began in my home town (St. Thomas, Middleton in Spring Garden, Jamaica). I'm a mother, grandmother and the last child of 10 children of my parents. I was only 11 when both my parents tragically passed away. This left me in a state of shock because I was only 11 years of age. At that that young age, one will think one's parents will be around for a very long time. It was very distressing to wake up knowing that my dad and mum are no longer there. It was like a dream which I hoped to wake up from but, this never happened.

After our parents passed away, my big sister (Tootise) took me in and looked after me until I was 18 years of age. During my time at my sister's I was not really interested in school work because I found it hard to concentrate in anything academic—it was a hard and challenging experience but I managed with what I could.

Whilst a lot of girls my age took into academics, my love and joy was music. Majority of my spare time was spent learning new songs and modeling. In fact, i was so involved with music such that people in my area called me "THE REGGAE SUN SPLASH". At that young age (18), I formed a group called "CULTURED SISTER" with my best Friend (Honey) who later moved to the USA.

I came from a music-loving family so I wasn't surprised at my dedication to learn music and investing most of my time on becoming better at what I do. Aside from music, I also was heavily involved in church activities and supporting charities in my community.

In 1977, I entered into a talent show of which I won. In that same year, I recorded my very first album (I'M STILL IN LOVE WITH YOU BOY) which went to No. 1 on the Chart. It was the very beginning of a great and successful journey for me. My brother (Busta Pearson) is an inspiration for me in terms of music success. In the same year I recorded a new album with another music group (IT'S OF 77) and we got to No.1 on chart too.

Some of singles include; Wily Wily, How you Lovin So, Settle Steady, Handsome and the list goes on. I thank God for giving me this great talent and also the successes I have enjoyed.

In 1984, I got married to an incredible man who made me feel so special. After so many years together, he sadly passed away which was another blow on my person. Life challenges can either make us or break us but we have to choose what will serve us in the future. I never thought my husband will be taken from me at that age but I continue to soldier on knowing that, one day it will get better. My faith in God was my main source of strength and all the prizes and awards I have won in my life so far cannot be compared to God's love for me. Finding Christ is my biggest achievement in life.

I later re-married but things did not work out with my second husband so, I'm currently focusing on reviving my music careers and supporting others to shine especially charities.

Our health is our wealth says a wise person. My health was challenged when I was hospitalised and had a cataract operation. I also overcame this life changing difficulty through prayers, support from good friends and my family. I never knew how strong I was until after a won this battle.

I spent most of my time promoting my business and supporting other people. I have since rebuilt my life and looking forward to the future opportunities.

My suggestion to anyone out there who is thinking of giving up on their dream is; "You have to continue until you win."

Many times in our lives we give up even before we begin our journey. We also allow others to change our direction because they don't believe that we can make it without their support.

Steps to reaching your goal and awakening the giant within you are;

1. Identify your personal and professional goals
2. Understand what you really want to pursue first
3. Take action towards making your dreams happen.
4. Love yourself
5. Follow your path and pursue your dreams
6. Seek God's help.

There is no harm in dreaming big and going for GOLD

Sasha Capocci was born and brought up in Morocco. She has spent the past 30 years in Britain, where she is a mother of two children, one of whom is blind and hemiplegic as the result of hospital negligence at birth.

Sasha is much involved with her local Rotary Club and NSPCC and fundraises for several other charities.

A year ago, she helped set up and run the Visually Impaired Club, which runs weekly meetings, with socialising and activities for adults, recognising that their social needs are ignored by social services.

Email: sashacapocci@hotmail.com

Chapter 20
Holding on for my little Angel

Sasha Capocci

M y name is Sasha. My journey began when I was in the delivery room for the birth of my first child. The original hospital I was booked into—where I was familiar with all the nurses—could not take me. They had no water supply and would not have been able to perform an operation had I needed one, so I was transferred to one of the West London Hospital.

It was July 1986 and I was by myself in a big room in the maternity department, which was closing down that summer. I was in labour for 36 hours, but staff only came to check on me infrequently. After 36 hours, I was made to have the baby by normal delivery because they did not want to give me a Caesarean section. I remember the midwife was due to finish her shift around 7pm. She gave me the oxygen and stayed till 8pm. Another midwife took over, but there were complications. She was on her own and kept calling and buzzing for help, but no-one came. Thank God my husband was there to help her out because I was in pain the whole time.

By 1am, I delivered my baby and suddenly we saw a doctor and another nurse come to help. They took the baby to clean him up. However, he didn't cry—there was no sound. I didn't see him until a few hours later, when a social worker came in to explain why my baby was in the special care unit.

Apparently the umbilical cord was wrapped around his neck during the birth, which left him deprived of oxygen. He suffered brain damage, hemiplegia and blindness.

To be told that your small bundle of joy will never see is devastating. It is a huge shock to the system and we needed time to come to terms with it.

I have endured horrible times—seeing other children with sight, comparing them to mine, seeing pity in people's eyes. But what none of them know is that having a child with visual impairment can open up a whole new world to enjoy.

Looking back at the early years as I do now from time to time; some very special moments stick out in my mind and because I have a very special child indeed and I'm grateful. There were knocks and bumps, but that was a part of the learning process. I was there for Michael, to hold his little hand, as he went to nursery, and then to a special primary school.

Years went by, and I realised that his special needs school was not giving him the learning and the education I was expecting from it. So I took him out of school and educated him at home—it was the best decision I have ever made.

Before your special needs child goes to school, he has to go through an assessment which will decide how and what he is taught. But how can anyone assess a child they have known for no more than five minutes?

I always trusted my instincts and I was always persistent. I reminded myself that I am the one who knows my child best and I live with him 24/7, compared with a visit lasting just a few minutes from a medical professional.

The lives of parents like me is already complicated enough—without adding in a fight with the authorities. But that didn't stop me. For me, when one door closes, seven others open.

When I took Michael out of school, we learnt together. We have five senses and one of them is missing for my little boy. But the others are enhanced; sound and smell, especially, are very important to him.

When we are out and about, I describe myself as a commentator—I am his eyes. For my son, I have made sure my perfume has been the same for the past 27 years. Unfortunately, nowadays, I have difficulty finding it as it is only available in two stores, but I still make sure I get it. I personally like wearing dark colours, but sometimes I wear orange because this is Michael's favourite colour—and the colour of his bedroom and his bathroom. Yes, he is blind, but he can see some colours. When you think of being blind, you probably imagine total darkness. A small number of blind people cannot see anything at all, but most can still see light, dark and shadows, and identify some colours, although usually nothing very clearly.

After such a traumatic experience during labour, which almost cost my baby's life, I started helping other mothers in the same situation. Having a child with a disability involves going into another world, with another language and another way of living. Each family that has been chosen to have that special child has a blessing from God. God is testing us and we must try our hardest to succeed in our mission.

When Michael was nine, I launched a charity for the blind in Barnet, called Barnet Look. I ran it for 12 years before leaving it to parents with smaller children to take over.

We were told that Michael would never be able to read braille. But he proved everyone wrong and now can teach it to others. I remember when he was young, his sister used to be jealous of him because he could read in the dark. At his grandmother's funeral this year, he stood in front of everyone at the church and delivered a beautiful speech, which he read from braille.

My little Angel is now 27 years old. He is a man and he is educated. He is a technology fanatic, and can even repair computers. For many years, Michael has used software on his computer that talks to him, so he can use his laptop as quickly as you or I could. He is always on hand to offer his friends advice on which new gadget they should try or which mobile phone contract they should have. He also loves languages and learning new details about other countries.

I always take Michael with me wherever I go to; I want him to be part of society and I want him to know how to function in different settings and to see the world. He is very musical, he is part of two choirs and he plays tennis for the blind. I take him to places where he can learn the social skills he needs—I feel that I must help him be more productive rather than make him more disabled.

And let's stop thinking of blind people as just blind—they are people with feelings, needs, desires and dreams, just like all of us. Every day, we learn something new. We can see ten things with our eyes in one second, and it will take me five minutes to describe it to Michael. Yesterday was the first time that he touched someone's very long beard and he had a fit of laughter: how come someone has got a pony tail on his chin?

One of my fellow Rotarians runs a talking newspaper and decided to open a club for visually impaired people. So I grabbed the opportunity with both hands. I am very pleased to be a part of the club, which is nearly one year old and doing wonderfully. I help run the group, fundraise and adapt games so that they are suitable for everyone. I make people experience how blind people feel by putting blindfolds on them. The majority of people feel unsafe, dizzy, uncomfortable and scared.

I have also played a game myself, pretending to be blind. I wore the blindfold at home and I bumped into things, but after 30 minutes, I could adjust and learn to live without my sight. Importantly, I found ways to learn and play with Michael.

While writing this, I am reminded of a beautiful essay that a close friend of mine introduced to me. Welcome to Holland, by Emily Perl Kingsley, explains the experience of raising a child with a disability.

She compares preparing to have a baby to planning a fantastic holiday to Italy.

"You buy a bunch of guide books and make your wonderful plans to places like The Coliseum, The Michelangelo David and The gondolas in Venice; you may learn some handy phrases in Italian. It's all very exciting. "But the plane lands and the stewardess comes in and says,

"Welcome to Holland." You must prepare for a different life in a different place. You have to get new guide books and learn a completely different language.

Kingsley writes: "You begin to notice that Holland has windmills . . . . and Holland has tulips. Holland even has Rembrandts.

"If you spend your life mourning the fact that you didn't get to Italy, you may never be free to enjoy the very special, the very lovely things . . . about Holland."

Having Michael has brought me into contact with so many wonderful people I may otherwise never have met and together we have had the most beautiful experiences. For us, every day is a learning day.

Did we give up? No! Was it easy? No! But then the best things in life are never easy.

Conclusion

"The power of faith will often shine forth the most
when the character is naturally weak."
—Augut Hare

We got there in the end!

Their stories say it all. These women have been through pain, rejection, illness, loss, fear, low self-esteem—everything that could have prevented them from shining their lights for the world to see. Rather, they chose to stay unbeaten to the knocks life threw at them.

No wonder a wise man said, "It's not the blowing of wind that determines your destination, but the set of the sail."

The reason is that the wind blows us at every point in time, but our choices make all the difference. Certainly, the wind blew on all these individuals whose stories we have read. What sets them apart is their persistence to remain focused on the endless possibilities that life has to offer.

"Everywhere is a walking distance if you have the time."
—Steven Wright

We are all on a journey of discovery, and we are responsible for the results we achieve in the process. It doesn't matter what situation you may find yourself in right now; there's another chance to start again. Even the smallest change can make all the difference.

Never give up on your passion, dream or goal to do, have and become more. Remember you are the designer of your life and the choice is up to you.

"Yesterday is a cancelled check, today is a gift and tomorrow is a promise."

However, the past is a great teacher if we look hard enough and take lessons from yesterday's experiences.